HATCHET, HANDS & HOE

Planting The Pioneer Spirit

HATCHET, HANDS & HOE

Planting The Pioneer Spirit

A Bushel of Practical Nostalgia
by Erica Calkins

The Caxton Printers, Ltd.
312 Main Street
Caldwell, Idaho
1996

Library of Congress Cataloging-in-Publication Data
Calkins, Erica,   1959-
    Hatchet, hands & hoe : planting the pioneer spirit : a bushel
of practical nostalgia / by Erica Calkins.
            p.   cm.
    Includes biographical references (p.   ) and index.
    ISBN 0-897004-372-2 (alk. paper)
    1. Gardening--Oregon. 2. Gardening--Oregon--History.
3. Frontier and pioneer life--Oregon.   I.   Title.
SB453.2 07C34   1996
979.5'041--dc20   96-5681
                                                                  CIP

Printed and bound in the United States of America by
The Caxton Printers, Ltd.
Caldwell, Idaho
161159

To
My mother, who encouraged my writing,
Bemaw and Granddad, who inspired me,
and
The Spirit of the Pioneers that live on in their plants.

About the Illustrations

Several sources and mediums combine in the illustration of *Hatchet, Hands and Hoe*. It is the author's intent to combine visual elements common during the Oregon Trail and Victorian eras with more modern and colorful representations of plants and gardens as they can be recreated in our time.

The author has gathered images from books published in the 1800s, as well as from antique merchandise and seed catalogs, and hundred-year-old seed packets and fruit labels. Where the source is known, abbreviated credit is given with the illustrations, with complete source information listed in the bibliography.

Drawing upon the author's research of pioneer garden plans, artist Teresa Sales has created colorful garden plans. These are found in the color section in the center of the book. Ms. Sales also illustrated and designed the book cover.

There are numerous historic photos throughout the text, and their sources are credited where they appear. All other photographs are by the author, including the full-color photos of plants and flowers in the center of the book.

A Word of Caution

Many wild plants have chemical properties dangerous to humans if improperly used. It is often difficult to tell "good" plants from their poisonous cousins. Some plants that grow wild also may have been treated with dangerous pesticides or weed control chemicals.

    NEVER eat wild plants or use them as medicine without first consulting a qualified plant expert and/or your doctor. When selecting varieties to plant, check with your County Extension Service to determine if any are considered noxious weeds in your area.

CONTENTS

Preface xi

KITCHEN GARDENS
Produce and Poultices..................................1
Recipes 22
Kitchen Garden Plan...............................29

NATIVE AND NATURALIZED PLANTS
Weed Walking 31
Recipes 50

DOORYARDS
Medicinal Plants.......................................53
Recipes 56

FIRST FRUITS OF THE LAND
Fruit-bearing Plants Come West..................59
Recipes 75

EMIGRANT MEMORIES
Their Favorite Flowers...............................77

ROSES OF THE OREGON TRAIL............................93
Appendix: Garden Recreations 107
Bibliography...121
Index 125

Color Illustrations and Garden Plans..........following 50

The American West in the Nineteenth Century

"A FAMILY ON ONE OF THE OVERLAND TRAILS...IN THE 1870s,"
The Frenzeny and Tavernier illustration first appeared in *Harper's Weekly*, April 4,
1874.

PREFACE

LIVING HISTORY isn't structures or costumes but a way of interacting with the past; and what could possibly be more living than our gardens? The stories in this book are nostalgic, but they also call all of us to preserve the past in a practical way. Remembering is so very important—it is the tie that unites families, communities, and cultures. Wisdom and encouragement from the past strengthen us to face the challenges of our own future.

I plant zinnias every year because my Granddad did. When their bright colors explode, I sense his warmth and strength in my garden. When my "Bemaw" came to our home as a hospice patient in May, my first rose of the season flowered. When she died, just a week later, all my roses were in bloom. Our family has decided to save that early rose, no matter where we go. To us, it will always be the "Bemaw Rose."

Every family has those special people whose stories need to be saved and shared. The pioneers left behind many such stories. It is my privilege to bring them to you with the hope you will start new family traditions based on this rich legacy from the past.

There are those who believe that history should not be presented with emotion; feeling colors the interpretation, somehow. However, the words in this book have been purposely selected—with feeling—to convey a sense of the times. Although the vernacular of the pioneers may be considered inappropriate in our day, I have chosen to use it, nonethe-less—for these are their stories.

This book is not meant to be a scholarly dissertation, although all information presented has been thoroughly researched from letters, diaries, and early historical works. Still, remembrances can be faulty, and information incomplete. (Napoleon wrote that "history is only an agreed upon set of lies.")

If these stories touch you, perhaps you will be inspired to study, preserve, and participate in history—even if every anecdote cannot be authenticated. Please join me in this adventure of practical nostalgia: an idea I like to call, "Planting The Pioneer Spirit."

Erica L. Calkins

"THE GOLDEN PUMPKIN, NUGGET OF THE FIELD"

Farm Festivals

HATCHET, HANDS & HOE

Planting The Pioneer Spirit

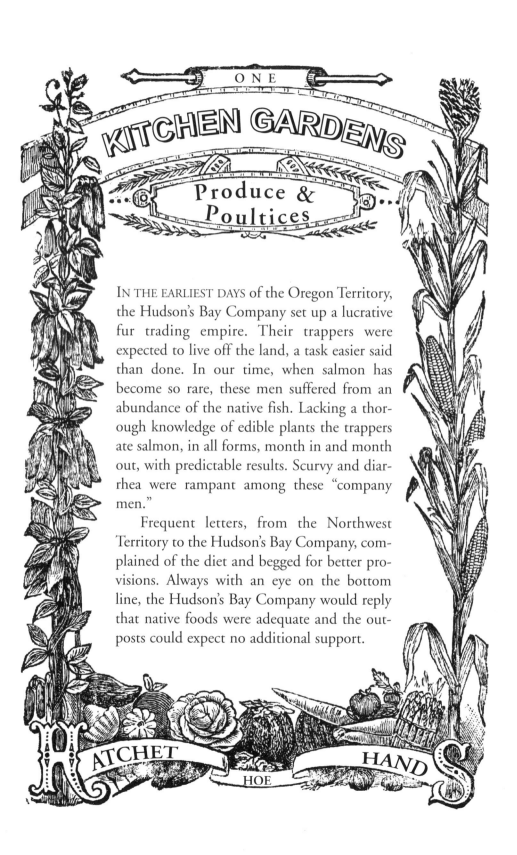

ONE

KITCHEN GARDENS

Produce & Poultices

IN THE EARLIEST DAYS of the Oregon Territory, the Hudson's Bay Company set up a lucrative fur trading empire. Their trappers were expected to live off the land, a task easier said than done. In our time, when salmon has become so rare, these men suffered from an abundance of the native fish. Lacking a thorough knowledge of edible plants the trappers ate salmon, in all forms, month in and month out, with predictable results. Scurvy and diarrhea were rampant among these "company men."

Frequent letters, from the Northwest Territory to the Hudson's Bay Company, complained of the diet and begged for better provisions. Always with an eye on the bottom line, the Hudson's Bay Company would reply that native foods were adequate and the outposts could expect no additional support.

HATCHET HANDS

HOE

CARDOON AND LEEKS
The photo depicts Fort Vancouver's winter vegetable garden.

Finally, one particular letter must have touched the heart (if not the innards) of the Hudson's Bay Company owners. In it, one man was recorded as having evacuated his bowels to a measured distance of six feet. Clearly, something had to be done to improve their diet. (One also wonders if the trappers were suffering from boredom. Whom do you suppose was measuring?) Grudgingly, the Hudson's Bay Company sent their outposts seeds so they could raise their own crops—and the future settlement of the great Northwest Territory was secured.

Cabbage, onions, potatoes, carrots, and similar hardy foodstuffs were grown at the Hudson's Bay Company forts. Not all the fortresses were blessed with good soil or gardeners but Fort Vancouver, under the leadership of Chief Factor Dr. McLoughlin, would point the way to the future.

CARDOON

Dr. McLoughlin was not a typical company man—characteristically, a company official had an eye only for profit. Of Scottish ancestry, McLoughlin was compassionate, visionary, and an avid gardener. Ships' captains, knowing of his great horticultural interests, would bring Dr. McLoughlin seeds and plants from the Spanish Missions and Sandwich (Hawaiian) Islands. A large kitchen garden for the "gentleman's table" was grown along with fruiting trees and shrubs.

Oregon Trail Varietal List

Beans

Oregon Giant—Old Oregon variety listed in Beans of New York, had other names in past

Scarlet Runner—Pre-1850s, listed on Hudson's Bay Company archives seed list, 1855–1870; a favorite of Thomas Jefferson

Beets

Mangelwurtz—Very old, used in Europe as stock feed, edible as young beet, listed by Burr, Vilmorin

Broccoli

Purple Sprouting—Old British overwintering type, pre-1835

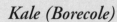

Cabbage

Early Jersey Wakefield—An American selection of the English Early Wakefield, since the 1840s

Quintal D'Alsace—Old French late cabbage, listed by Vilmorin

Carrot

Chantenay—Similar to Early Market Horn, mid–1800s

Cucumber

Early Russian—An old pickling type, listed on Hudson's Bay Company requisition lists 1855–70

Kale (Borecole)

Ragged Jack—Pre-1877, listed in Hudson's Bay Company archives

Marrowstem—Very old, listed by Burr, Vilmorin

Leek

Carentan—From 1874, listed in Vilmorin

Lettuce

Tennis Ball—Pre-1804, grown by Thomas Jefferson

Melon
Pike—Cantaloupe (muskmelon) brought over
    the Oregon Trail

Mustard
Colewort—Seed is from Scotland, bred there for
the Hudson's Bay Company to be grown in the Pacific Northwest

Onion
Large Red Wetherfield—Listed by Burr,
    Vilmorin and Hudson's Bay Company
    archives 1855–1870, apparently popular at
    the time

Pepper
Bullnose—One of the oldest "bell" type known,
    Hudson's Bay Company archives 1855–1870

Squash
Small Sugar—Early pie type

Boston Marrow—Winter type listed by Burr
    and Hudson's Bay Company archives
    1855–1870

Vegetable Marrow—Apparently used either as
    summer or winter type; Burr and Hudson's
    Bay Company archives

Blue Hubbard—Also called "Hubbard", listed
by Burr, Vilmorin

Tomato
Large Early Red—Popular market
    tomato in Minnesota during the
    1850s and 60s, cross between Large
    Red and Early Red

Yellow Plum—very old

Cardoon
A very old spring vegetable, stems are blanched for eating

Courtesy James Dalton

FOR RELIABLE SEEDS GO TO

Courtesy Oregon History Center

"CABBAGE LADY"
This fanciful beauty promoted the Clay & Richmond Seed Company of
Buffalo, New York.

As the missionaries arrived, they admired and copied the example of self sufficiency set at Fort Vancouver. Narcissa Whitman and Eliza Spalding were the first white women to make the overland journey. Their party was also the first to successfully bring a wagon through. Actually, this first wagon had been reduced to a cart by journey's end, but it carried needed supplies—including seeds—and set the pattern for all the wagon trains that followed.

Narcissa Whitman, in her diary, recalls the joy of eating an apple after the long months on the trail. Jokingly, she also related that it was "the rule of the Fort" not to waste a single seed. She coined the saying from a humorous incident involving a gentleman who had recently arrived from London by ship. While dining at the fort, the visitor pulled some seeds from his vest—leftovers from his last meal in England—whereupon Dr. McLoughlin "confiscated" the seeds to plant in his garden.

The planting of produce, begun by the Hudson's Bay Company, was the foundation for long term survival in the territory. Missionaries planted gardens, as well, but at first many of theirs were complete failures. They complained often of the difficulty in doing spiritual work when the pressures of survival were so great. Time was the enemy—the endless work breaking both spirit and body. But patience, prayer, and persistence ultimately allowed the missionaries to mimic the successes of Fort Vancouver. The ladies at Mission Bottom (Jason Lee's enterprise near Salem, Oregon) described the making of pumpkin pies in letters home.

One son of a missionary described his first year in the territory as only a child could—from his stomach. Breakfast, he said, was bread and molasses; lunch was the same; and for variety, the dinner table featured molasses and bread.

Survival for the emigrants that were to follow was also very different from the lives of the trappers and company men of the Hudson's Bay Company outposts. Without a large and powerful company to support them, they had to "make do" with what they brought.

To set the scene, imagine fall in Missouri. Harvest is done. Potatoes, cabbages, carrots, and beets are root cellared; apples and pumpkins dried; sacks of corn and beans stacked—with a little extra put aside for the overland journey to Oregon the following spring. Through the long, cold months the family eats their "winter" food. Then spring arrives, and the six–plus month trip across the Oregon Trail begins.

Always on the move to stay ahead of winter's pursuit, trail food had to be quick and easy to prepare. A pot for coffee and a single Dutch oven for baking might serve as many as ten travelers at a sitting. One especially resourceful cook, Mrs. Scott, related "cooking for sixteen men with only one frying pan in which to bake all the bread and fry all the meat, and one tin bucket in which to boil and bake the beans and make the tea."

Day in, day out; bread baked, bread fried; beans on lay-over days for a relief from the monotony. Cooking anything with only sagebrush or prairie anthracite (buffalo dung) was quite the challenge. Dried fruit, fresh meat, and wild greens (called vegetables out of place by some emigrants) were rare treats—rating special note in diaries.

Those who came by ship didn't necessary fare any better. One gentleman who got stranded at the Isthmus of Panama for a month complained that he was "thoroughly tired of eating monkeys and yams."

Families arrived in Oregon City in the late fall, facing another, much leaner winter. Most had only a bit of wheat—not enough to survive through to the spring. At Fort Vancouver, the generous Dr. McLoughlin could not bear to see the women and children starve—he

Harnessing the Waters

In order to have an effective millrace, the stream might often have to be deepened. Slow and tedious dredging was avoided by damming the stream. When the dam was broken, the resulting flood often scoured the stream bottom to the necessary depth for the mill wheel to be installed.

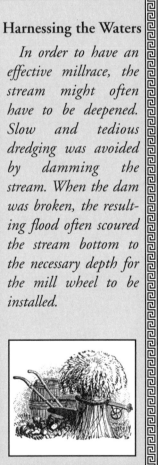

"lent" the newcomers provision for the winter. But his compassion would be his undoing with the Hudson's Bay Company. Not only his benevolence, but his model of successful agricultural practices allowed the emigrants their foothold in the territory—ultimately leading to the Americanization of the Northwest and a loss of British influence. Sadly, even when the settlers were secure on their donation land claims, they rarely repaid Dr. McLoughlin's loans.

It was a long, wet, first winter for those early emigrants. They would boil wheat, after tediously cleaning it by hand, for up to twelve hours in lye water to make a kind of hominy. The puffed wheat filled bellies and stretched supplies. They would also parch the wheat and grind it to make a coffee substitute.

The settlers didn't usually make a "to-do" about surviving, but one account captures the starkness of their early months by its simplicity. A nineteen-year–old bride wrote, "We could only buy enough [wheat] to boil, glad to have that, in fact...we became very fond of boiled wheat, it tasted so strong of money...by economizing closely we lived through the first winter." Folks with dried peas lived similarly.

But finally, spring arrived. Seeds from home, so carefully packaged for the journey, were unwrapped—seeds that had grown overnight in the minds of emigrants, talking and dreaming of the rich Oregon soils as they sat around evening fires along the trail. One old woman, child of an early settler, recorded a story that speaks volumes about the hunger for fresh food and the importance of gardens. It's about Mamma, her cucumber seeds, and the old family rooster—Dominick.

It was finally the day for Mamma to plant her quarter–acre kitchen garden. Bringing out her seed papers and hoe, she prepared to plant. Of all her seeds, she was proudest of her cucumbers.

Courtesy Clackamas County Historical Society,

"MAMMA'S HELPERS"
The charming, unidentified gardeners were captured in a studio portrait.

In fact, she had already promised seeds to other ladies on the wagon train after harvest. In that time, when you made a promise, your word was your bond—a very serious commitment. Now, Mamma had two young daughters and it was their job to keep the chickens away from the newly planted seeds. The chosen day was long, warm, and beautiful—and the children (being children) forgot their task and turned to play. Suddenly, remembering their charge, they looked on in horror to see the saucer where Mamma's precious cucumber seeds had been. There was Dominick, the old family rooster, downing the last one—gulp. What could they do?

Well, they didn't have any choice but to frantically call out to Mamma. Running from the field, all hot and sweaty, she saw immediately what had happened. Looking her girls straight in the eye, Mamma tells them with a cold, stern voice, "You go catch that rooster now, you hear?" So the girls rounded up old Dominick while Mamma went into the house to get Papa's straight razor, a needle, and thread.

With determined step and tone she commanded, "You hold that bird down on the block. Stretch his neck and don't you let go, hear? Don't you let go!" Wincing, the girls stretched out his neck and Mamma slit his throat from stem to stern; pulled out the cucumber seeds; sewed him up and went back to planting.

Fortunately, the story has a happy ending. Dominick lived to sire many more little chicks, and Mamma had a good harvest—with plenty of seeds to share with her neighbors. And do you know what? After planting that quarter-acre kitchen garden, she was much too tired to punish the children.

Kitchen gardens were planted "hard by" the cabin and surrounded by a rough picket fence for extra protection. Even with all the care they received, it often took two years to harvest any food. Deer took their toll as did the native neighbors. The Indians, with their generous traditions, didn't understand the concept of private ownership and felt anything growing on the land was for the good of all. They often exchanged foods of their own but it was small comfort to the ladies who were trying to re-create their old homes on the raw land. Neighboring livestock and the wild longhorns that roamed the valley were also constant threats to any garden.

PURPLE-FLOWERING
RASPBERRY

First gardens were usually cleared and roughed out with a hoe. Sometimes a plow could be borrowed but tools were in short supply. (One pioneer family, the Matheneys, smoothed the roughened sod for planting with a harrow made of a thorn bush.) The kitchen garden provided all the fresh "garden sass" for the family—greens, root vegetables, winter squashes, beans, and occasionally a special treat or two like tomatoes or popcorn. Berry and fruit bushes, such as currants or gooseberries, were planted around the perimeter.

The emphasis was not only on fresh eating, but also on what could be preserved and stored through the winter months. Yuletide decorations in the Oregon's Aurora Colony would include dried beets hung as ornaments on Christmas trees. However the "average" settler, if there was one, would hang gifts on the tree and root–cellar their vegetables.

Many plants also served double duty as home cures. A strong decoction of carrots was gargled as a cure for the "putrid sore throat" (diphtheria). Onions boiled down with a little sugar made a thick syrup, a treatment used to ward off and cure respiratory complaints. These old varieties of onions were far more potent than their modern cousins, and the active sulfur compounds that give onions their tang acted as a natural antibiotic. Although they didn't know it, the settlers created a very effective sulfa-drug with their onion syrup. The "pie plant," or rhubarb, was a common staple—not only for pies, but in stewed form it was administered for stomach aches.

Tobacco was grown to smoke, but it also made an effective poultice for killing fungus. These cures were often hit or miss. The carrot decoction was useless, as was a suggested cure for measles: tea made of dried sheep droppings.

Culinary herbs were not very popular until later, although the Yankee ladies did grow sage to add to their soft, white farm cheese—not only for flavor, but as an aid to digestion. Sage was also used as a rinse to brighten dulled hair and when steeped as a strong tea and mixed with honey, sage was a "sure" cure for canker sores when held in the mouth as long as possible.

Hops were a particularly useful plant, not for beer making (that came later), but for yeast making. Hops contain a preser-

Great Balls of Fire

Smoking was one of the few treats settlers had. Even women smoked. Old illustrations of "nooning" on the trail, portray women with their corncob pipes. Lighting one's pipe did call for ingenuity however. Matches or "sulfur sticks" were too expensive for daily use. A magnifying glass might be used out in the field but most common, if away from the hearth, was a "ball of fire." A long strip of rag was lighted and then rolled into a smoldering ball. When you needed a light, you'd unroll the rag strip, blow on the end to create a flame then light your pipe. Pockets often had holes burned in them from careless smokers.

TOBACCO

vative resin. When boiled in water and strained, the hop water can be added to bread or yeast starter to keep it fresh longer. Hops also have the happy quality of being a sedative. Hop tea, though incredibly bitter, was much appreciated after a 4 AM-to-midnight day in an eight-by-eight cabin. Hop pillows were also made to aid sleep. (I've tried this, and the first night or two the effect is very pleasant. But as the hops lose their fresh-ness, they begin to smell very much like dirty feet. Perhaps this wasn't as noticeable in those earlier days). Entire families picked hops once the industry began in earnest. With hops

BURLEY TOBACCO

HOPS

SERIOUS-LOOKING HOP YARD CREW
After putting in a long day's work, they are obviously enjoying a moment
of silliness, adorning themselves with hop garlands.
Courtesy Clackamas County Historical Society

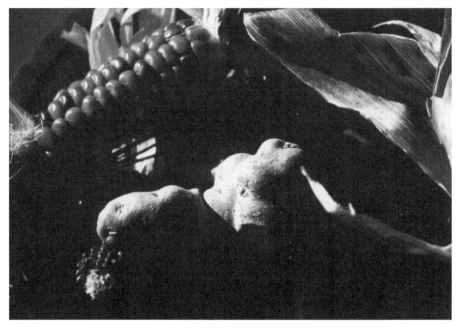

MANDAN BRIDE CORN AND HAIDA POTATO
The corn dates from the Lewis and Clark Expedition; the potato was
traded by Spanish expeditions to Pacific Coast Indians

being such a powerful sedative, pickers would be very relaxed after working in the fields all day. An interesting side effect was that in nine months after harvest, there was usually a baby boom among the families of happy hop-pickers.

Potatoes were a particularly important crop. Since wheat was the currency of the valley, it was not an item to be consumed carelessly. Thus, potatoes and cornmeal were used more than wheat flour in breadmaking. Potatoes were also attributed with saving lives. A staple for the settlers, they were also a favorite with the native folks. As settlement expanded, so did conflicts between the emigrants and the Indians. Settler's homes, known to have stores of potatoes on hand, were spared destruction—the Indians not wanting to waste the precious food. Potatoes were also used to bring starts of favorite plants west. Cuttings were stuck in the potato which provided food, water, and protection.

"Makin' do" took many forms for the emigrants. Tinware for cooking, eating, and particularly in the form of milk pans, was highly prized. One gentleman got tired of his plates disappearing while away from his cabin. He quickly solved the problem by nailing them to a plank table. Whenever he wanted to clean them, he simply turned the table over, swept them off with hot water and put the table back. One wonders whether the doubtful cleanliness of his dishes also deterred potential pinchers.

Milk pans, used for letting cream rise, were probably one of the most critical pieces of kitchen equipment. In a day when we watch our fat intake so carefully, it is hard to understand the importance of fat in the pioneer diet. Without any other convenient source, butter was a staple for cooking and calorie intake. (In fact, cooking grease was in such short supply that women on the trail had to scavenge fat from the intestines of dead oxen—in order to have enough grease for

Thundermug Revenge

The Chinese were well known for their bountiful gardens. Their produce was much prized, especially in the gold towns of the West. Unfortunately, their foreign ways were not as appreciated. In John Day Oregon, some of the boys from town persisted in stealing produce from the Chinese, enjoying their ill-gotten gains as they bragged about their feats.

One early morning, before dawn, the pack of boys were poised to strike again when they saw the Chinese gardener leaving his shack and heading for the garden. Seeking out his prized melons the Chinese gentleman dumped his full thundermug (chamber pot) around the plant and returned inside.

Nauseated, the boys suddenly realized the source of fertilizer for the garden and never again touched another melon.

Wild Cow Milking

If necessity is the mother of invention, hunger is certainly the mother of courage! The need for milk and butter caused more than one woman to brave the terrors of finding, subduing, and bringing home one of the wild longhorns first introduced at Fort Vancouver. These feral cattle roamed the roads terrorizing early settlers. They were also free to any brave enough to catch and tame them.

A husband and wife would rope a cow, tying its feet together, and then leave it for several days until nearly starved.

Returning for the cow, they led the subdued creature home where it was hobbled for a few more days, allowed only a little food from the hand of its new owners. At last the cow would be trained to milking by the wife sitting on her stool with the husband standing at the head with a huge club—in case the cow should object.

cooking.) A hole in the family milk pan was a serious matter.

One day, a ship pulled into Oregon City and several ladies went to meet it in hopes of finding replacement tinware. There was not a milk pan to be had but there were a number of chamber pots. So the ladies eyed the pots, thought about milk pans, and bought the stock out. One little girl, recalling the incident as an old woman, related that she "felt squeamish about butter so produced but it worked as an acceptable substitute."

Let me close this chapter with a story that reflects the diligence, care, and perseverance by which the pioneers lived. One of the early settlers in Clatsop County, Oregon hailed from Kentucky. With her came a handful of flax seeds (the plant's fibers are spun into linen), carefully carried over the Oregon Trail. Now in Kentucky, it was the custom to plant flax on Good Friday. So, on that day, the woman went to her field with hatchet, hands and hoe (the only tools to survive the journey) and her handful of flax.

Cutting the sod with her hatchet, she carefully laid aside the squares. Then she worked the soil, as best she could, with her hoe. Finally, because the flax seeds were so small and fine, she worked out all the clods and bumps with her hands. Planting each slippery, tiny seed with care, she smoothed the soil and patted them gently in. Now, above her claim, some native American gentlemen assembled to watch the "doings" of their new neighbor. Day by day they watched, as she weeded and hauled water. At last, the day of harvest arrived. Incredulous, they watched

'Round and 'Round the Mulberry Bush

Although wool and linen were the primary fibers used by the settlers, the Matheney family recalls that many women would keep silk worms for thread making. These worms can only feed on mulberry leaves making these a popular shrub in the settlement days.

HATCHET, HANDS AND HOE
The author displays the most common pioneer gardening implements.

as she pulled her precious flax up by the roots (the fibers from which linen is spun run the entire length of the plant).

Then, she did the most amazing thing. She threw her armfuls of flax in the pond to rot! Well, they laughed and they laughed, figuring she must have gone crazy from all her hard work. They didn't know that flax has an inner core which must be rotted before the flax can be carded and spun for fiber. That season she had enough thread to pad the first quilt in Clatsop County and a quart of seed to plant the following year. Winter passed, Good Friday arrived, and again she repeated her ritual with

Healing Flax

Flax was valued not only for linen but for its medicinal properties as well. When cooked or warmed, the seeds break down into a mucus mass. This was valuable for making poultices to draw out infection. Flax seeds were also placed in the eye to draw out foreign objects.

hatchet, hands and hoe. Her Indian neighbors gathered, not believing she would do this all over again. But by the end of that second season, they weren't laughing at this woman. They were trading with her, because they had learned the value of this fine fiber for their fishing nets. She became rather a wealthy woman, in her own right, trading linen thread for barrels of salmon.

This story is not so much about one woman and her flax, but the qualities of care, discipline, and perseverance that were passed on to her child, Dr. Owens–Adair who became one of the first women physicians in the Territory. The title of this book commemorates that early emigrant and the seeds of a Good Friday planting that transcended generations.

Kitchen Garden Recipes

Pumpkin Butter

Fresh fruit was unavailable in the winter, but that didn't stop cooks from being creative. This recipe is super on pancakes, sourdough cornbread, or even with meat dishes. Any winter squash, fresh or canned can be used, and it is an easy way to add a healthy vegetable to your diet.

1 medium size squash
2 Tbs. apple cider vinegar
1/4 c. molasses
cinnamon, nutmeg, cloves, fresh ginger to taste
3/4 to 1 c. brown sugar

Take your squash, prick it, and put it (whole) in the oven to bake at 350 degrees until soft. Remove from oven and let cool. Scoop out the meat into a bowl. Add all other ingredients and place into greased casserole dish. Bake slowly at 250 degrees until firm. Leftovers can be kept in a covered container in the refrigerator for up to three weeks.

Pan–Fried Cabbage

Chop up one small cabbage, one large onion, one clove garlic, and one fresh apple. Preheat fry pan, add 2–3 Tbs. lard (or olive oil if

you insist on being healthy). When fat is hot, add vegetables. While cooking, add salt, pepper, and a bit of sugar to taste. You can also add a splash of vinegar if desired. Remove from heat while cabbage is still slightly crunchy. Serve immediately.

Farm Festivals,

Cake Presses

There was no such thing as cookie cutters in territorial times. Instead, designs were made to order through the local tinsmith. These cake presses were much larger than a cookie cutter and were often handed down as a family heirloom.

The Aurora Colony museum, in Aurora, Oregon, features a large, elegant rocking horse cake press.

Hop Water Gingerbread

Gingerbread is a classic recipe, used for centuries. The addition of the hop water makes the dough chewier, lighter, and imparts a very delicate flavor. (Hops were used a number of ways besides cooking: the fiber as a flax substitute, dye, wax, and sheep fodder.)

1/3 c. boiling water steeped with one handful hops and strained

1 Tbs. baking soda

1/2 c. milk

2 1/4 c. molasses

3/4 c. butter

3/4 Tbs. (approximately, to taste) freshly grated ginger

2 tsp. cinnamon (optional)

dash of vinegar (optional)

4 1/2 c. whole wheat, white, and graham flour (mixed)

Blend together all dry ingredients in large bowl. Cut butter into dry ingredients and blend thoroughly. Add molasses then pour in boiling hop water and stir. Thin with milk to a thick batter consistency. Pour batter into 2 greased 8–or 9–inch pans. Bake at 300 degrees for 45 minutes. Test by inserting knife into the center. If it comes out clean, the gingerbread is done.

A Little Taste of Heaven

Treats were truly treats for a settler's child. One boy recalled the kindness and generosity of a teacher. While reading the story of the gingerbread man, it was revealed that this lad had never tasted gingerbread. In the Christmas spirit, the teacher took his student to a bakery in Oregon City and bought him some. The boy thought surely that this must be food fit for the gods. How good it is to remember a time when kindness was common and gratitude for simple pleasures abounded.

Yeast Making

Bread has always been considered the staff of life. Although baking powder (saleratus) biscuit like breads were common; light, fluffy

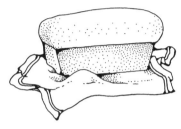

yeast breads have always been preferred.

Yeasts come in many forms; sourdough, sponge or cakes. Sourdough is a liquid yeast medium that contains wild yeasts found naturally in the air. The sponge is also a liquid leavening that uses cultured yeast. Yeast cakes are a dry form that also contain cultured yeast.

Yeasts are tiny microorganisms that create the spongy texture and beloved bready flavor. As bread rises, these "critters" multiply. As the yeasts "breathe," they give off a gas, CO_2. This is what creates the little pockets in the dough. Once the bread is baked, the yeasts die but the wonderful smell and texture of fresh bread remain.

Since bread was made many times a week, the thrifty cook would make her own yeast; using and renewing it constantly.

Stove Lore

Most settlers cooked on an open hearth for many years. Some stoves miraculously made it over the trail but generally, a cookstove was considered a great and coveted luxury.

Developed by a Massachusetts inventor Benjamin Thompson (later Count Rumford) in the late 1700s, the wood cookstove was in universal use by the 1860s. In his initial work with indirect heating, he used materials on hand while stationed at Fort Golgotha, site of an old cemetery. The recycled gravestones worked admirably for his ovens but every loaf of daily bread was inscribed with the name of the deceased.

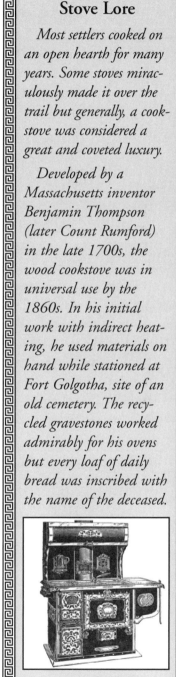

> *Stoves were such a rarity in the territory that many had never seen one.*
>
> *One little girl recalled visiting a neighbor and sitting on a pleasantly warm chair. Her mortified mother pulled her off and chastised her for sitting on the stove.*

Sourdough

Make a mixture of flour and water about the consistency of pancake batter. Let sit in the open for a couple of days. The wild yeasts in the air will colonize the mixture. You'll be able to tell because it will bubble and expand. For a more consistent flavor, mix the flour and water as before but introduce a packet of dry starter. Pioneers often traded yeasts, enjoying the different flavors.

You can add a little sugar to feed the growing colony but it takes away some of the sourness. Some folks also add a little vinegar for a sharper flavor. The yeasts also grow better in a more acid environment. Once your starter is foamy, pour into a glass container and refrigerate until needed. It's best to use it at least weekly but I've kept mine going if I use it twice a month or so.

When you want to use your sourdough, pour some out in a bowl, add flour, a dash of sugar and warm water until it begins to foam again (activates). Different flours can be used for different flavors.

Farm Festivals,

Dry Yeast

Place 2 c. hops in 2 quarts water and boil for 30 minutes. Place 4 c. flour into a stoneware container, pour boiling hop water over the flour stirring constantly. Let mixture cool until tepid. Dissolve 1 packet dried yeast in 1 c. warm water and 1 Tbs. sugar. (You can use a cup of sponge or sourdough starter instead of dried yeast).

Set the mixture in a warm place to ferment. Stir down periodically until mixture doesn't rise any more. It may take a couple of days so cover to exclude dirt, etc.

When the fermentation is complete, add cornmeal until the dough is stiff enough to knead. Roll or pat out dough about 1/4" thick. Cut into circles and dry thoroughly, turning while drying. I have also filled greased muffin tins half full with the mixture to dry. Turning is very important to ensure the cakes are completely dry. Discard any that have mold. A constant, even heat is best, under a wood stove or on a dehydrator works best.

One cake of yeast will make one loaf of bread. As in the old days, you'll need to let bread rise overnight or activate the yeast cakes with warm water and sugar an hour or so before baking. These will keep indefinitely in the freezer.

The Hot Seat

The Applegate family had a regular visitor; an Indian gentleman who would enter their cabin without knocking, sit to be fed and then leave—never saying a word. It became so common, the family ceased to think about it. After a year at their claim, the women finally sent the men to Oregon City to fetch home a wood cookstove.

Quickly installed, the stove was immediately put into service. As usual, their native neighbor paid a silent visit but chose to sit in the warmest place in the cabin—the stove—which was still quite hot.

Pausing only a moment the Indian leapt up, still silent, and rushed out of the cabin never to be seen again.

BORAGE
The blossoms are pale blue to lavender.

Kitchen Garden Plan Notes

All the plans presented in this book are original designs based on the Heritage Gardens planted at the End of the Trail National Historic Site in Oregon City, Oregon.

Done in the style and plants of the time, they are a composite of many family traditions. Any one garden would probably not be so aesthetic, those folks were just too busy.

For exact spacing and cultural requirements refer to the *Sunset Garden Book* series or contact your local County Extension office. In some cases exact varieties have not been indicated on the plan. The appendix contains some lists you can work from as well as sources for ordering plants.

Planting gardens with heirlooms serves a very important purpose. Many of these old varieties are becoming quite rare. With the focus on modern hybrids, the gene pool has been dangerously reduced. Many of these plants are extraordinarily hardy and their seed can be saved from year to year, unlike hybrid varieties.

Not only will you enjoy a measure of self sufficiency but you'll be protecting a valuable resource, as well.

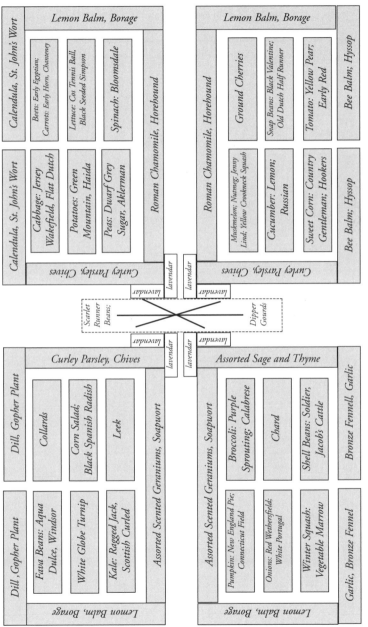

Pioneer Kitchen Garden

SCAR ON A PINE
The injury was caused by wagon axles scraping through the pass at Blue Mountain Crossing.

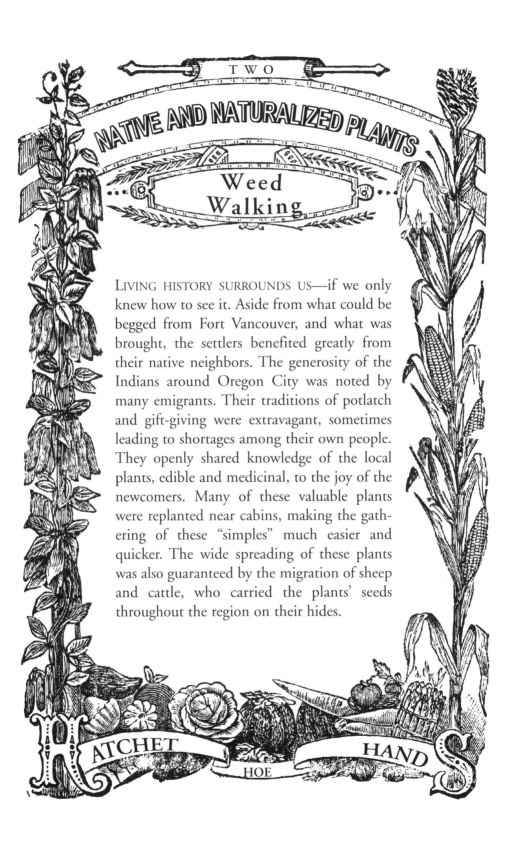

TWO

NATIVE AND NATURALIZED PLANTS

Weed Walking

LIVING HISTORY SURROUNDS US—if we only knew how to see it. Aside from what could be begged from Fort Vancouver, and what was brought, the settlers benefited greatly from their native neighbors. The generosity of the Indians around Oregon City was noted by many emigrants. Their traditions of potlatch and gift-giving were extravagant, sometimes leading to shortages among their own people. They openly shared knowledge of the local plants, edible and medicinal, to the joy of the newcomers. Many of these valuable plants were replanted near cabins, making the gathering of these "simples" much easier and quicker. The wide spreading of these plants was also guaranteed by the migration of sheep and cattle, who carried the plants' seeds throughout the region on their hides.

HATCHET HANDS
HOE

How To Know The Wild Flowers

WILD YARROW

The white women in the community who had herbal knowledge earned the respected title of "Aunts" while among the Indians, the same position was called *tla-quill-augh.* Among the native Americans there would be three or four of these general utility folk able to set bones, assist as midwives, and gather healing plants.

Every housewife had common plant knowledge, but true herbcraft was considered a "darkling" thing. In the Appalachian traditions herbalists were known as "yarb" or "witch" women, carrying a sense of danger and suspicion. When crises arose, however, folks gladly traded their fears for cures. The Applegate women were exceptional in their knowledge and use of herbs. After the tragic drowning of

"HEAL-ALL," *PRUNELLA VULGARIS* CLUMP

two of their boys in the Columbia River below The Dalles, the women of the family prepared a pudding using wild rose hips they gathered. What an interesting response to grief. The meal not only helped bind the survivors together, but rose hips are very rich in vitamin C: known to help reduce the effects of stress. Later, when settled at Yoncalla, Melinda Applegate used pokeberry paints to record scenes from their lives on the back of old maps.

How To Know The Wildflowers.

PAINTED TRILLIUM
Trillium erythrocarpum and fruit

Knowledge of healing plants was passed freely back and forth between the two peoples through the women-folk. Although professional botanists, like Townsend, came early to the territory, the studies of these "grass men" weren't widely available to the average settler. The ladies learned to use trillium and blackberry leaves as birth aides, fir needle tea for fevers; heal–all

There's Danger in Them–Thar Plants!

As much as I encourage folks to experience living history for themselves, I'd be remiss in not warning of the dangers of self medicating with plants. Identification is crucial, many healing plants look remarkably like their deadly kin.

Besides that, there is the problem of dosage and allergies that might be unique to you. The pioneers made do but many of their methods were questionable at best.

Please kids, do not try this at home!

LOW CUPPED PLANT MINER'S LETTUCE

(which unfortunately doesn't cure a darn thing) and yarrow (or the soldier's plant) to staunch the flow of blood. Yarrow's properties as an anti–coagulant were particularly important in reducing bloody diarrhea, a serious and common problem. Cascara, or chittim bark, retained its value as a laxative for many years. (It was considered the "aluminum can" of the depression era, when children gathered the bark for sale to pharmaceutical companies.)

In the late spring, when the sap was up, a common cough syrup was made from the bark of the wild cherry. This reme-dy was also fortified with alcohol, ensuring its popularity

Courtesy Clackamas County Historical Society

PROTECTING A PRECIOUS BERRY HARVEST
The unidentified pickers look on in stoic approval..

among the menfolk. Pine pitch, with its antiseptic turpen-
tines, was used as a curative on wounds. It was also a favorite
with children who chewed it as a gum. Scurvy was allayed by
field nibblings of miner's lettuce, sheep sorrel, and oxalis while
chickweed comforted skin eruptions and was given internally
for asthma. Some native Americans would place miner's lettuce near an ant nest. After the ants had crawled over it, they
were shaken off and the green was imbued with the tang of
formic acid from the insects.

CAMAS BULBS AT BLUE MOUNTAIN CROSSING

Oregon Grape roots were used as dye, throat gargle, and a general tonic for that tired, run–down feeling. Salves were very important home cures. A common one was prepared in the spring by cooking down a mixture of June butter and "Balm of Gilead" (cottonwood) buds. June butter was considered especially medicinal, as the cows were eating all the healthy

Salves

For modern purposes use 5 parts olive oil (as it will not go rancid) to 1 part melted bees wax. Heat the oil with your choice of plants, and let sit 3 or 4 days. Strain and reheat oil to a warm temperature, and combine with warm bees wax.

EQUISETUM—HORSETAIL FERN

simples and new grass in the fields. Rough, bare feet were particularly appreciative of this salve since shoes (being too expensive) were rarely worn, except in winter. Mutton tallow could be substituted but it made a much harder salve.

Elderberry blossoms would be gently sautéed in butter as a salve for the eyes, or batter–dipped and fried to eat. (In the spring, children would make popguns and whistles out of the new shoots.) Without easy access to doctors, these basic plants, and many more, provided practical as well as psychological support for pioneer families.

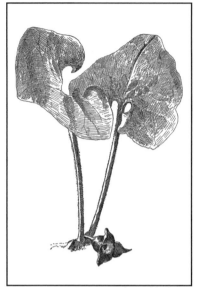

WILD GINGER

The value of native plants went well beyond medicine; many were used for cooking and basic housekeeping, as well. Obviously, berries of all kinds were gathered. A late summer jam was made from the Oregon grape combined with salal berries. Camas, a staple for Indians, was also eaten by the pioneers. Mrs. Whitman told of the sweet, fig–like flavor of roasted camas. Others would bake the root into a pie: the Northwest version of a New England pumpkin pie.

Unfortunately, the newcomers didn't always have the same concern for preserving their natural resources as did the native Americans. Some of the settlers in the Blue Mountain region of Eastern Oregon, allowed their hogs to forage in the camas patches, ruining them for all. The loss of this important food caused the local Indians to rise in violence against those wasteful settlers. Most emigrants were thrifty, however. Cooks learned to curdle cheese using nettles instead of rennet and "peppered" food with the seeds of shepherd's purse. Pots were scrubbed with sand and the horsetail fern, which contains glass-like silicon in its fibers. Furniture was also fine-sanded with this useful plant. Young mothers happily discovered they could pack baby bottoms in moss and wild ginger (to reduce the odor). The fresh scent of ginger leaves were also appreciated in homemade soaps. Gentlemen who went a-courting relied on wild ginger to keep their stomachs from impolite and embarrassing rumbling. Fresh cedar bark was valued for its ability to repel fleas (a bane of repeated comment in Lewis and Clark's journals). Widely used as

MULLEIN STALK AND FLOWERS

cooking vessels, hollowed cedar logs might also serve as babies' beds (though not the same ones).

The children of the settlers were very quick to learn from their native peers. They discovered licorice fern, a treat that grows on maple or alder trees. The flavor is best in late spring when the sap is rising, giving it a sweeter flavor. Roasted, these roots were also made into a cough remedy.

TRUE TANSY, WITH VIBRANT YELLOW BLOOMS

MULLEIN LEAVES

Games using native plants were widely played. Quileute boys would compete in a breath endurance game using sword ferns. Holding a frond upside down, they would take one deep breath and repeat "pila, pila, pila...." while pulling off the individual leaves one at a time. The winner was the boy who pulled off the most leaves in one breath.

Where pine trees grew, children could make dancing dolls. By taking a small stem of pine and trimming the bottoms evenly, these could be made to dance by placing them on a thin sheet of bark and tapping underneath with the fingers.

There was an interesting tradition among the Indians around Oregon City involving fir trees. When a young man proposed to the lady of his choice, he would find a young fir and split it to within a foot of the base. If done properly, this "marriage tree" would heal and grow into two separate trunks on a common base, boding well for the couple's future life. If the tree didn't survive, it was a sign they should reconsider— although many young men found another tree to try again.

Indians would mark their trails by bending young trees and pegging them to the ground. This was very helpful to settlers who used the same paths prior to the building of roads proper. Rarely, one can still find these trail trees growing in undisturbed woodlands.

The settlers, in their turn, introduced useful plants from eastern homes. Mullein was smoked to clear the lungs (or used as stuffing in tattered shoes and quilts). An oil made from the mullein flowers was a popular remedy for earaches while a tea, steeped from the leaves, was prescribed for kidney ailments. Violet tea cleared phlegm, while tansy (not to be confused with the poisonous tansy ragweed) tea was prescribed for rheumatism. Actually, tansy didn't do a darned thing for the rheumatism, but it is a mild narcotic and probably made the sufferer feel a mite better. Tansy was also taken as a wormer while fresh tansy was kept in the pantry to ward off insects. its natural properties as an insect repellent ensured its place in

DANDELION

CHICORY

many a coffin as a very traditional burial plant.

Dandelions were widely planted as one of the healthiest greens of spring. A doctor's wife in Oregon City went so far as to plant a bed of dandelions thirty feet long by ten feet wide. Dandelion wine was also popular, although frowned on by the "Good Intent Society."

Comfrey, or the protein plant, was very important both as fodder and as a cure for many complaints. It does contain a compound called allantoin that speeds healing of

A HONEY BEE VISITS LAVENDER-FLOWERING COMFREY

external injuries. Chicory and clover are also remnants of live-stock foods. Chicory was occasionally roasted and added to coffee to stretch supplies (the secret to the famous coffees of New Orleans). The lowly plantain has the very important quality of stanching blood and contains a natural antibiotic. Used in hospitals during the Civil War, this plant followed western

How To Know The Wild Flowers

BOUNCING BETTY OR
SOAPWORT

migration and was known among some native Americans as the "English-man's Footsteps."

Thistles were introduced as a natural host for wild yeasts, an important quality since the settlers couldn't shop for necessaries. The native thistle roots were roasted in firepits and eaten by the Indians. Lewis and Clark's journals record that prepared this way, the roots were very sweet.

Bouncing Betty, or saponaria, was widely planted and can still be seen naturalized east of the Cascade Mountains. A very mild soap was made from the roots, a process involving pounding then soaking them. This gentle solution was used for washing babies, hair, and underdrawers—much preferable to the sometimes harsh lye soap.

In addition to weeds, many wildflowers were also introduced. Pioneer mothers brought the ox–eye daisy as a cure for

Saponaria Suds

The foamy nature of this plant caused those of Pennsylvania–Dutch descent to add it to their homemade beers to give the brew more head.

Housewives had a more mundane use however, its soapy nature also worked wonders as a laxative.

POPPY

fevers and the tiny bellis daisy (commonly found in lawns) just because it was pretty. Daisy-chain–making was a favorite pastime of pioneer girls in the spring. Foxglove was known to help the heart, but little girls liked to put the bell-like flowers on their fingers as fancy mitts. Lonely Scots, from North Carolina, bountifully planted Scotch Broom. Its lasting, cheerful flowers and hardy constitution made it a favorite with the ladies—who also fashioned hearth brooms from the stems. New brooms had to be made each year. Tradition had it that if you swept with an old broom into the New Year, the head of the household would be swept away (die).

Dr. McLoughlin also appreciated the beauty of flowers. California poppies, one of his favorite varieties, were allowed to naturalize freely. Descendants of these cheerful plants still blan-

How To Know The Wild Flowers

WILD ASTER
While not favored by the ladies, the very similar Michaelmas daisy was.

Honeysuckle Sipping

DAISY GRANDMOTHER
A simple game for children of all ages: trim the petals from a large daisy to
make a bonnet. With a pencil, rub off the pollen to make a face.

ket Washington roadsides in the summer. As the Hudson's Bay
Company trappers retired with their "country" (Indian) wives
to French Prairie near Champoeg, Oregon, they took seeds
from Fort Vancouver with them to their new farms.

Bachelor buttons were among the most popular wildflowers
and became so widely grown around
French Prairie that they were known in
Oregon City as French Pinks. Farmers had
a less fond name for these flowers: hurt-
sickle. The tough stems of the bachelor
buttons would blunt the large "cradles"
used for wheat harvesting.

There is a wonderful story of a little
girl who loved her daddy—and bachelor

BACHELOR BUTTONS

buttons. When Papa came in at noon for supper, a couple of buttons were missing from his jacket. It was a chilly day, and he asked Mamma to sew the buttons on. But she was in the middle of a chore that couldn't be left. As Papa sat and ate his supper, the little girl slipped his jacket off the hook and oh, so carefully sewed on two blue bachelor buttons.

When done, she secretly replaced the coat on its hook and waited for Papa to finish his supper. Rising to return to work, he reached for his coat and there were the bachelor buttons next to the expectant face of his little girl. With a kiss, he gently "buttoned" the jacket—secretly chagrined at her choice of flower but warmed by her love.

It's remarkable to realize how our roadsides and lawns are so filled with history, yet so little appreciated. For those of us who fall behind in weeding, we can always claim the excuse of historical preservation, thanks to the pioneers.

Farm Festivals

"WITH SUN-TROD FACES AND HORN-GLOVED HANDS"

Recipes
Using Native and Naturalized Plants

Tansy Mulled Wine

Popular as a flavoring in Elizabethan times, tansy has long been used as a medicinal. Many healing plants were mulled in wine to make them more palatable. Recent studies have indicated tansy may be carcinogenic, so use restraint.

Place 4–5 leaves and a blossom head of tansy in 1/2 gallon of sweet, white, or red wine. (I find it works best if I pour the wine into an open-mouth jar first).

Warm the wine until just above tepid in the oven or microwave. *Do not boil.* Serve immediately while still warm.

The wine will be infused with the bitter–sagey flavor of tansy, a real taste of the past.

How To Know The Wild Flowers

TANSY

Native and Naturalized Plants

Castor Bean—Poisonous

Trillium

Chicory

Foxglove Digitalis

A

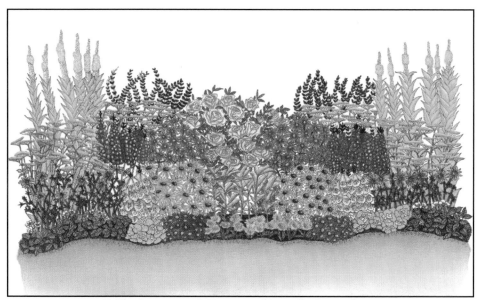

Native & Naturalized Border

Native & Naturalized Border
Shade to Partial Shade

B

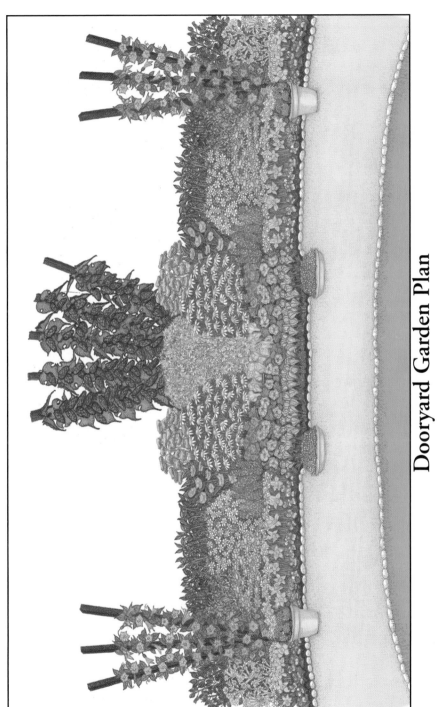

Dooryard Garden Plan

C

Dooryard Plants

Monarda, Bee Balm, or Oswego Tea
Earl Gray, the tea favored by colonists after the Boston Tea Party, derives its unique flavor from this common, yet-valued plant. Its crimson petals attract bees and hummingbirds.

Rose Scented Geranium
Cuttings were planted and saved each year. A tender perennial, its required care further endeared it to the ladies. Sometimes planted indoors in boxes as a room freshener. (*Cake recipe, page 56*)

Horehound
A beautiful green-silver plant grown for sore throats and coughs. When boiled, it produces a very bitter, brown flavoring. (*Candy recipe, page 56*)

America variety Sweet Peas
These fragrant flowers were a "must" at any entrance door, where their sweet scent was appreciated.

D

Dooryard Plants

Clarkia

This bright pink wildflower was named for William Clark, co-captain of the Lewis and Clark Expedition.

Sweet Rocket

Sweet fragrance coupled with long-lasting bloom made this beauty a favorite.

Evening Primrose

No known medicinal use for the time, but it was hardy and pretty—a perfect pioneer plant.

Snapdragons

A classic dooryard flower and a favorite with children. The blossoms make wonderful finger puppet puppies.

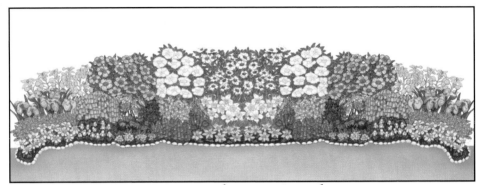

Spring Flower Border

Summer Flower Border

Emigrant Memories—Favorite Flowers

Wall Flowers and Golden Saxifrage

Lilac

Black Hollyhock

Fushcia, Hardy

Lupine

Nora Barlow Columbine

G

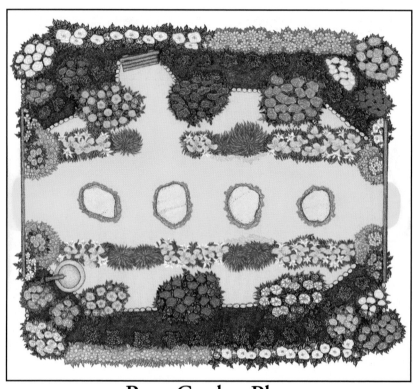

Rose Garden Plan

Pioneer Roses

Following is a list of pioneer roses, with special thanks to Janet Witter. Although reasearch continues on exact varieties, this list is a good start. Available photographs are included.

Pink Sweetbrier—*R. eglanteria* pre–1551, once blooming.
Pink Moss—*R. centifolia or Salet*, 1854, repeat blooming.
White Moss—*R. centifolia,* unique and unidentified variety in Lone Fir Cemetery *(photo, page 80).*

Rosa Mundi "God's Rose"
R. gallica versicolor pre–1581, once blooming.

Old Red Moss
R. centifolia or William Lobb, 1855, once blooming.

Harrisons Yellow
Hybrid foetida, 1830.

Centerfolia

I

Pioneer Roses

Austrian Yellow—*R. foetida* species, once blooming.
Rambler Seven Sisters—*R. mutiflora* 1817, once blooming.
Rambler Old White Memorial or White Lady Banks.
Rambler White and Yellow Lady Banks—*R. banksiae* 1807, yellow 1824, once blooming.

Austrian Copper or Persian Copper
R. foetida species, once blooming .

Persian Yellow, or Persian Gold
R. foetida species, once blooming.

Persian Copper and Persian Gold
Together they create a fiery burst of color..

J

Pioneer Roses

Father Hugo—*R. hugonis* introduced from China 1899, once blooming.
China Hermosa—China Hybrid 1840, continuous bloom.
Apothecary Rose—*R. Gallica pre*–1600, once blooming.

Queen of the Prairies
R. setigera hybrid 1843, once blooming. The photograph is of a cutting taken from Lone Fir Cemetery in 1970.

Crested Moss or Pink Moss Rose
R. centifolia Chapeau de Napoleon (Napoleon's Hat) 1826, once blooming.

China Old Blush
China 1752, repeat bloom.

Old Cardinal

K

Pioneer Roses

Rosa Multiflora white rambler type—*polyantha thurbengii,* 1830s, once blooming.

Pink Damask

R. damascena or Autumn Damask, pre–1819, repeat bloom. Photo is at Josephine's grave (see page 110).

Rosa Alba

Probably Madame Plantier, 1835, once blooming.

Red Alpine

Dog Rose

L

Dandelion Wine

A healthy drink, full of the taste of summer.

Gather a gallon of heads. *Do not get the tiniest bit of stem in with the flowers.* They contain a bitter resin that will ruin the wine. Pull off the petals with one hand while holding the green base of the flower head with the other.

After removing the petals, place in a glass jar or food grade plastic bucket and add three quarts of boiling water.

Let stand, covered, for seven days stirring at least once a day. At the end of the week, strain out the petals, reserving the liquid into a clean glass or plastic container.

Boil 1 1/2 pounds sugar and/or honey in another pint of water, cool and add to dandelion water along with one packet of wine yeast and the juice of two lemons. Cover and let ferment another seven days.

At the end of the second week pour off the liquor, leaving as much sediment behind as possible, into a clean glass or plastic container. Boil another 1 1/2 pounds sugar and/or honey in one pint of water, cool and add to the liquor.

Let ferment until no more bubbles are being produced (about another week). Bottle and seal the liquor for at least six months, preferably a year, before drinking.

The true lesson here is that patience has its rewards. The pioneers enjoyed the fruits of their labors and understood the virtue of waiting for them. If you make this an annual rite of spring you can enjoy a continuous supply of this special wine. Settlers also favored its use for cooking small animals i.e. squirrels, birds and frogs.

Bon Appetite!

Garden Plan Notes
For Native And Naturalized Plants

Native plants are part of the flora that were present in the ecosystem prior to the emigration of the pioneers. Naturalized plants were introduced from trading ships, Hudson's Bay Company forts or emigrants. Often the introduced plants did so well, that modern observers would assume that they've always been a part of the natural landscape.

The success of these plants lies in their hardy nature. Sometimes they thrive to the point of being a nuisance but for the gardener with little time this can be a perfect garden.

Requiring little in the way of weeding or fertilizing, these plants are an excellent choice for back-of-the-property screens or areas for attracting wildlife.

Although many of these plants can be collected from the wild, unless they are threatened be a good steward—and don't. Disturbing plants in their natural habitat sets a bad example and might inadvertently destroy a plant or habitat of value. Growing from seed or purchasing plants from a reputable nursery, enables you to select exactly what you want and gives you the choice of planting some slightly tamer varieties appropriate for a smaller, home landscape. *(See color plate B.)*

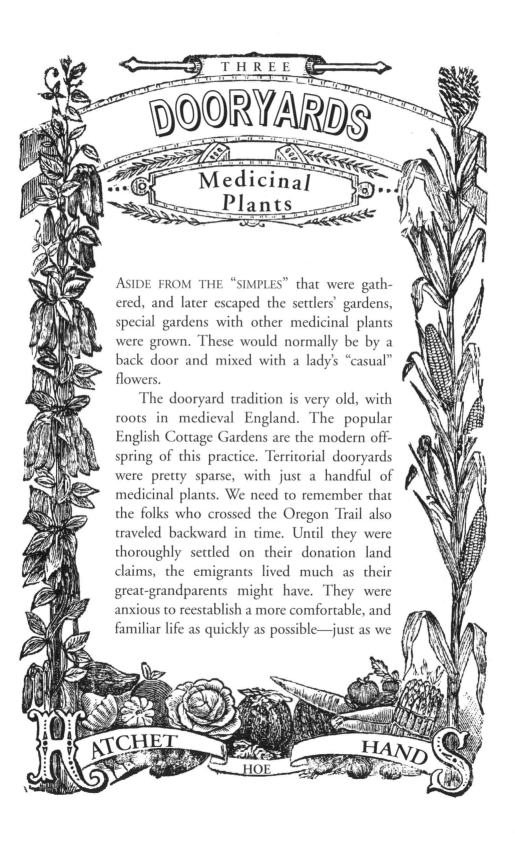

THREE

DOORYARDS

Medicinal Plants

ASIDE FROM THE "SIMPLES" that were gathered, and later escaped the settlers' gardens, special gardens with other medicinal plants were grown. These would normally be by a back door and mixed with a lady's "casual" flowers.

The dooryard tradition is very old, with roots in medieval England. The popular English Cottage Gardens are the modern offspring of this practice. Territorial dooryards were pretty sparse, with just a handful of medicinal plants. We need to remember that the folks who crossed the Oregon Trail also traveled backward in time. Until they were thoroughly settled on their donation land claims, the emigrants lived much as their great-grandparents might have. They were anxious to reestablish a more comfortable, and familiar life as quickly as possible—just as we

HATCHET
HOE
HANDS

would. This meant using doctors, buying medicines, and living in a fairly modern fashion. The use of plants in healing was considered old-fashioned by many but necessity and caution ensured that some medicinal plants were brought along. The Sisters of St. Mary's skillfully combined the traditions of natives, pioneers, and current science to offer doctoring to all who came. In the dooryard one might find potherbs like calendula or marigolds set among mints, lavender, horehound, chamomile, and feverfew. Purely decorative flowers like johnny-jump-ups, daylilies, and jonquils were added for a touch of beauty.

Courtesy Clackamas County Historical Society

KITCHEN GARDEN
An unidentified family surveys the bounty, growing alongside their cabin.

MARYLHURST MEDICINE

In an old grade book are handwritten notes and medical remedies belonging to Sister Mary Laurentias (Lila P. Kellogg). Known for her healing skills, Sister Mary was a true angel of mercy to those who came to her for help in the late 1800s. The following are excerpts from her book of cures.

SNAKEBITE AND BEE STINGS:

Slice an onion in half crosswise and place on wound. In five minutes the onion will turn green then place the other half on the wound. It will take two to three onions to cure. Remedy should be applied at once. If the wound is three to four hours old, cauterize with silver nitrate and drink plenty of whiskey.

An alternate Indian remedy recommended "immediately applying a poultice of indigo (washing blue) and salt in equal parts mixed with cold water. Renew every two to three hours. Eat freely and drink tea of common blue violet."

DIABETES:

Make a strong tea of white birch and white pine leaves. Drink freely.

CARBUNCLES:

Mix wood soot with 2 oz. sour yeast batter, fine salt, castile soap and the yolk of three eggs. Apply the paste three times daily.

COUGH:

Saturate a lump of sugar with mullein oil and let dissolve in mouth.

PILES (HEMORRHOIDS):

Apply linseed oil (from flax) externally or inject.

FELONS (INFLAMMATION AROUND JOINTS):

Place handful each of tansy, hops, catnip and wormwood with small quantity tobacco and 1/2 teacup soft soap with water to cover. When boiling place blanket over vessel and place hand in steam. Keep it there up to 48 hours if necessary.

BLOOD PURIFIER:

12 oz. Honduras Sarsaparilla	*3 oz Yellow Dock*
4 oz. Wintergreen leaf	*4 oz. Burdock Root*
4 oz. Sassafras root bark	*6 oz. Dandelion*
4 oz. Elderflowers	*2 oz. Bittersweet*

Bruise all and add one pint each alcohol and water. Cover and sit in moderately warm place 3 to 4 days. Pour off 1 pint tincture, set aside. Add water to ingredients and boil. Pour off additional water and boil again. Then boil the two waters down to 1 quart, add liquor from the first. Add crushed or brown sugar and simmer until thick. Place syrup in bottle.

Recipes
Using Plants From The Dooryard

Horehound Candy

A great cough drop but also an old fashioned treat for any time. It is time consuming to prepare, but a big batch will last a year.

Put 4 c. water in a heavy bottom saucepan, add 1 1/2 c. horehound leaves. Bring to a boil slowly and simmer for 15 minutes, remove from heat and strain out the horehound leaves reserving the liquid.

Add 3 c. each white, granulated sugar and 3 c. brown sugar. Stir until dissolved. Boil to a hard crack. This will take 30–45 minutes. You will begin to see a color change when it gets close. Stir regularly to avoid scorching. If you have trouble with foaming, you can add a dot of butter. Use a candy thermometer or test by dipping a clean spoon into the mixture and let cool. If it hardens on the spoon, it is done. It will also form threads when dripped off the spoon when close.

When done, remove from heat and pour into an oiled, shallow pan. Mark the squares as soon as possible, break up as soon as the candy has set. Wrap each piece in wax paper and store in a dry place.

Rose Geranium Cake

This recipe was developed during the Civil War when sugar and flavorings were in short supply.

12 rose geranium leaves   3 c. cake flour
1 c. (2 sticks) butter   4 tsp. baking powder
1 3/4 c. sugar   3/4 c. milk
6 egg whites   1/2 c. water
1/2 tsp. salt

Rinse leaves. Wrap 6 leaves around each stick butter; wrap and chill overnight. Remove leaves; rinse and set aside.

In a large bowl, cream butter and sugar until light. Add egg whites, two at a time, beating well after each addition.

In a separate bowl, mix together all dry ingredients.

In a cup, combine the milk and water.

Alternately add the flour mixture and liquid to the butter mixture beginning and ending with the flour. Beat smooth after each addition.

Grease 2 large 9 1/2 inch round baking pans. Place 6 leaves in each pan and spoon the batter over. Bake at 350 degrees for 30–35 minutes.

Cool 10 minutes before removing from pans. Gently remove and discard leaves from the cake. Cool and frost with a light frosting of your choice.

FRONT YARD GARDEN
Pink roses, yellow lilies, black-eyed susans, and foxglove flourish with other assorted flowering plants.

Courtesy Clackamas County Historical Society

FIRST APPLE TREE

The original caption of this 1890 photo reads, "First Apple Tree ever grown on the Pacific Coast. It is still bearing fruit in the [Methodist] parsonage lot in Oregon City, Oregon. It is now over 50 years of age."

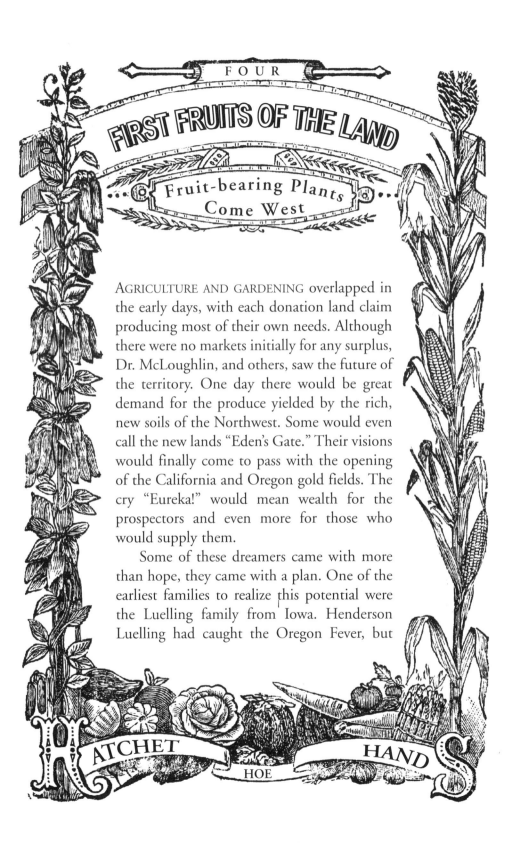

FOUR

FIRST FRUITS OF THE LAND

Fruit-bearing Plants Come West

AGRICULTURE AND GARDENING overlapped in the early days, with each donation land claim producing most of their own needs. Although there were no markets initially for any surplus, Dr. McLoughlin, and others, saw the future of the territory. One day there would be great demand for the produce yielded by the rich, new soils of the Northwest. Some would even call the new lands "Eden's Gate." Their visions would finally come to pass with the opening of the California and Oregon gold fields. The cry "Eureka!" would mean wealth for the prospectors and even more for those who would supply them.

Some of these dreamers came with more than hope, they came with a plan. One of the earliest families to realize this potential were the Luelling family from Iowa. Henderson Luelling had caught the Oregon Fever, but

HATCHET HANDS

HOE

Courtesy Clackamas Historical Society

LUELLING ORCHARD STOCK

The original handwritten caption of this historic photograph reads: "Best Side of Main Street, Milwaukie, Oregon, between Jackson and Monroe, 1900."

unlike many who simply cashed out and hoped for the best, Henderson prepared thoroughly. He was a second generation nurseryman and a Quaker. His father had been a physician, active in the underground railroad. Because of their beliefs, the Luellings were labeled "Black Republicans." (Later the family would name a cherry the "Black Republican" as a dig toward their old Iowa neighbors).

Henderson constructed a special "tree wagon" lined with lead and filled with a blend of Iowa soil and charcoal. Into this he placed some six hundred starts (scions) of quality fruit stock. In the spring, April 17, 1847, Henderson and a very pregnant Mrs. Luelling started across the Oregon Trail.

The two-wagon caravan was often forced to roll on alone in order to obtain enough water for their nursery stock. Travel routes and timing provided some protection for their cargo yet, in the drylands, the family would forfeit their own water for the trees. In the Blue Mountains of Oregon, special fires were built to keep the roots warm. Extra protection against the cold was provided by nesting the scions in family blankets. Mrs. Luelling complained in her diary that Henderson cared more about his trees than her.

Although traveling alone, the family was never troubled by Indian attack. Later, on arrival in the territory, the family heard through the "grapevine" that a war party had been poised to strike the lone family on the plains. As the Indians approached, they saw all the green, leafy starts in the tree wagon. With their great reverence for nature, the warriors turned away believing this family must be under the special protection of the Great Spirit.

Surprisingly successful, Henderson did lose about a third of his stock in an accident around Idaho's Snake River country, but all the rest survived and thrived despite the harsh conditions (as did his newborn son). Some of the trees grew as much as three feet in transit.

Arriving in November, the Luellings established their nursery at the site of the present Waverly Golf Course in Milwaukie, Oregon. Working from 4 A.M. until midnight daily, they were able to clear the land in a couple of months. They also got an enormous head start on their orchard by grafting their scions to existing "trash" trees. Settlers had been growing trees by using seeds from any fruits they ate. Many of these were of poor eating quality, but gave the Luellings lots of rootstock from which to work.

There is a story about the Reverend Waller's wife, who dried tons of apples, dumping the waste outside her cabin in the Oregon City area. Birds ate the seeds and deposited them liberally around the settlement in their droppings. The surviving seeds sprouted, producing hundreds of volunteer apple trees all around Oregon City. It's easy to imagine the Luellings using trees like this to help establish their nursery.

Within two years, they were able to take their first box of apples to the streets of downtown Portland. Seventy-five apples sold in only fifteen minutes for the unbelievable sum of a dollar apiece. Henderson's vision was vindicated. But the newspaper, the following day, pilloried Henderson—outraged at his "usury." Really, who ever heard of selling apples for the outrageous price of a dollar apiece? The incensed editors of the paper forgot the price the Luellings had paid to bring those "first fruits" through. Unsuccessful in whipping up citizen outrage, the demand only increased.

Henderson's brother, Seth, would later join the family and it was he who began the patient work of breeding and introducing new fruits. Henderson, ever a dreamer, moved on to California to establish a nursery fortune and industry there, only to lose it all later in a South American venture.

It was Seth who introduced the golden plum and improved rhubarb. He also introduced strawberries, but had to pull them from market for about ten years until the pioneer ladies learned how to use them. Well known for the breeding of cherries, Seth worked his huge orchard with the help of Chinese labor. His six–foot–two Manchurian foreman, Bing, was the undisputed boss of the fields.

One day, while inventorying new fruits, a wonderful new cherry was discovered. Seth's friends were so excited, they immediately asked him what he would name it. Thinking only a short moment Seth replied, "Well it's in Bing's row, we'll name it after him." And so, we've been eating Oregon history ever since: a living testament to the vision and perseverance of the settlers and the skilled Chinese labor that made their dreams possible. Cherries became a staple for housewives, using them in preserves, dried for winter and, of course, in pies.

One woman, known for her hospitality and cherry pies, was very clever about stretching her supplies. Sugar in the new territory was

Farm Festivals

abundant, coming over from the Sandwich (Hawaiian) Islands as ballast for ships in woven, grass sacks. Unfortunately, hard cash was not as plentiful. When visitors came, the gracious hostess would serve her famous cherry pie. The half she served to company had sugar—while the half served to family did not.

There is an interesting endnote to the contributions of the Luelling family. The two brothers, Seth and Henderson, had a terrible falling-out over the spelling of the family name. Being Quakers, Henderson considered it unseemly to have the long spelling while Seth wanted to preserve the original Welsh spelling. (Period accounts actually show at least five different spellings of the family name). The brothers ended their lives neither speaking to the other. In the ultimate irony, at the Milwaukie Pioneer Cemetery adjacent to the Luelling's old orchard, Henderson is buried under Seth's preferred spelling while Seth is under Henderson's. They also share, in death, a most fitting monument for these pioneer nurserymen. In the

RUBBING OF SETH LUELLING'S HEADSTONE

middle of the cemetery an old, old fruit tree umbrellas sweet white flowers each spring over the grave sites. Some forty feet high, it is a remnant, or at least first generation descendent, of those first tree wagon survivors.

Another early settler to grasp the potential of the territory was Phillip Foster. He had gone into partnership with Sam Barlow to operate the Barlow Road, a route providing emigrants an alternate to the deadly Columbia River raft passage into the valley. Facing the precipice of Laurel Hill, the emigrants would question the wisdom of their choice while lowering their wagons by rope with entire trees tied on the back as a break. When, at last, the exhausted pilgrims rolled in to Foster's place at the bottom of the Barlow Road, they were met with sweet water, meadows for their stock, and fresh produce.

Ever the entrepreneur, Phillip operated a restaurant, campgrounds, and a mill. He also packed salmon and peas for shipment to China, owned one of the first herds of branded (PF) longhorns in the valley, and sold nursery stock. Reaching

LUELLING FRUIT TREE
The old-timer flourishes in
the Milwaukie Pioneer
Cemetery.

Foster's Place was cause for celebration. The trail was finally over—Oregon City, and civilization, within "spitting" distance.

Two families who crossed together had daughters who had become inseparable, Mary Conditt and Nancy Black. On reaching Foster's Place, the girls couldn't resist exploring and left their mothers to wander about. Nancy and Mary came upon Phillip's orchard where some late peaches still hung. After months and months of winter and trail food, the temptation was just too great. Picking the fruit they sat and ate, and they ate, and they ate. Full at last, they returned to the wagons. Their stomachs, unaccustomed to so much fresh food, rebelled. In the night they were both struck with acute gastritis and died.

BARLOW ROAD TOLL GATE

Imagine the bitterness and heartbreak of those mothers. They had made it over the trail safely with their precious children. They came because of the bounty of the land, and in the end it was that very richness that killed their children. Nancy and Mary rest together, the first to be buried in the family cemetery at the Philip Foster Farm. A huge cedar tree towers beside their grave. When you bend to sweep the stone clean to read it, the smell of the cedar is

Terror at the Tollgate

The sheer terror of Laurel Hill, named for all the wild rhododendrons, can only truly be appreciated by visiting the site and peering up the scrabble track. At the bottom was Sam Barlow's original tollgate where settlers had to pay hard cash from their scant reserves. Their righteous indignation of having to pay for the privilege of surviving such an ordeal, caused Barlow to move the tollgate to the top of the road before the emigrants could vent their dissatisfaction.

Maps today indicate Tollgate right beside present Oregon State Highway 26. The gatekeeper, who lived at the toll gate and actually collected the money, planted two, magnificent elms to mark the original toll gate site. These died and were later replanted where they still stand commemorating the that last, great obstacle to the promised land, the descent of Mount Hood.

like sweet incense—a poignant reminder of these children. (Personally, I like to use this story as an object lesson on the importance of obedience for my children).

Phillip's partner, Sam Barlow, established his donation land claim at Barlow, just south of the present town of Canby, Oregon. Sam sold his claim to his son, William, who later married a southern belle named Martha Ann. Martha Ann, desperately missing her old plantation home, spoke fondly of its beautiful tree-lined drives. She spoke so often of the trees that William decided he would plant a carriage drive for her.

A family friend, Mr. Dement, who was returning East, was asked to bring back a sack of black walnuts and butternuts. Fulfilling his mission, Mr. Dement was delayed and passed the nuts to the next returning Oregonian, Mr. Thurston (the Territory's first congressional representative). While on ship, somewhere around Panama, Mr. Thurston contracted a fever and died. In that hot climate, the sailors were all in favor of

SAM BARLOW'S GRAVE
The epitaph reads,
"O do not disturb the repose
of the dead,
Behold the pure spirit has
risen and fled,
Nor linger in sadness around
the dark tomb,
But go where flowers
forever will bloom."

giving Mr. Thurston, and all his effects, a speedy burial at sea. Since Thurston was a congressman, however, the Captain considered that an unfitting end. Eventually, Mr. Thurston and his belongings made it ashore.

Unfortunately, Martha Ann didn't know this—and grieved intensely over the loss of the nuts. She mourned so long and so deeply that William, while on a business trip to San Francisco, made a special effort to track down the nuts.

Persistence paid off, and he indeed found all of Mr. Thurston's effects. Unfortunately, there was also a sixty-five dollar freight charge attached. William, ever the businessman, wasn't going to pay any sixty-five dollars for a sack of nuts. So, he returned home: nutless. In a move of questionable judg-

The Beginner's Reader

ment, he made the mistake of telling Martha Ann the story. Well, there was no peace to be found in the Barlow house after that.

William returned to San Francisco (can't you just imagine the muttering under his breath), paid the freight, and returned home. Reported in what must be a family account, William dumped the nuts triumphantly at the feet of Martha Ann. Cracking and savoring just a few before the parlor fireplace, they placed the rest in a box of soil, nestling them under the manure pile until spring.

BARLOW HOUSE
The wintertime scene features historic walnut trees that yet survive.

When the weather warmed, the box was pulled out of the manure pile revealing hundreds of tangled sprouts. Planted out in a nursery bed, the trees thrived and were finally given their place of honor: a four hundred-foot drive with carriage turn-around. Extras were given free to all the family, and the balance sold to a nurseryman for a profit of five hundred dollars. William probably didn't mind that sixty-five dollar freight charge too much in the end.

As "progress" cut into the Barlow claim, many of the old trees were removed. When the railroad came through, one of the great trees was dug up, loaded on two flat cars, and replanted in Portland. Highway 99 also took its toll, but about one hundred feet of the original drive remains. The Barlow family has left a living legacy throughout the Willamette Valley: the great black walnuts found from Portland to Salem owe their origins to Martha Ann's Virginia dream.

QUINCE

As the territory became more established, many kinds of fruits and nuts were brought. Quince was a standard not only for its fruit but as a beauty aid, as well. Crushed petals in the spring lent color to a girl's lips while the seeds of the fruit were boiled to make a hair-curling solution.

The Shipley family of Lake Oswego, Oregon were early growers of Concord grapes. Jams, jellies, and raisins were sold, as were "crocked" grapes. The fruit was loosely packed in a stoneware crock, covered with warm honey, then capped with

OLD FRUIT LABEL

an oil cloth. The natural yeasts on the grapes caused a mild fermentation that preserved the fruits for shipping. Grape leaves didn't go to waste either. They were used to wrap apples to keep them fresh for eating through the winter.

These "dainties"—jams, pies, fresh fruit, and such—played a special role in pioneer life. The long days of summer work and wet muddy winters isolated many families. Get-togethers, usually dances, would bring neighbors from miles around. Ladies would bring all kinds of foods: the most special being the "dainties" that rated a separate table of honor. These women were keeping hope and joy alive in their kitchens, by sharing their best with the community. The need for fellowship and food is captured in the satirical lyrics of "Oh Web Foot Land," set to the tune of "Oh Tannenbaum" (also the tune for "Beulah Land").

> I've reached this land of mud and rain
> And all its riches hard to gain,
> And once I've reached this very spot,
> Sometimes I wished that I had not.
> Oh Webfoot Land,
> Wet Webfoot Land
> As in my house I sadly stand
> And gaze throughout the dripping pane,
> I wonder when twill cease to rain.
> And once I've reached this very spot,
> Sometimes I wished that I had not.

Other Kinds of Garden Gold

With the temperate climate of the Willamette Valley, almost every possible crop was tried including cotton. The Sawtell family of Molalla came to the territory by ship packing their goods in the seeds of teasel.

Fullers teasel was raised as a cash crop for shipment to Europe where it was used in the processing of felt. The wild teasel is close kin to this useful plant.

Ginseng, usually thought of as an oriental plant, was a veritable mother lode of riches for growers in the Estacada, Oregon area. Brought from Ohio in the late 1880s, ginseng was widely grown for shipment to the orient until interrupted by World War I.

How To Know The Wild Flowers

GINSENG

APPLE BEES

Harvest times were rich with tradition, many carried over from early days in England. Work was made more fun by the playing of games and the gathering of neighbors.

Girls would twist the stems off apples saying the alphabet as they twisted. The letter spoken when the stem broke, was the first initial in the name of the boy she would marry.

Unbroken peels were thrown over the right shoulder and when they fell, the initial they supposedly made, indicated the intended.

Seeds from these apples were counted to divine the number of children the couple would have.

Seeds could also be picked out and carefully named, then plastered on foreheads. The seed that stuck the longest would be the name of a girl's true love.

Special suppers might be served from the three zones of the farmhouse; nuts from the attic, apples from the kitchen and cider from the cellar.

Honeysuckle Sipping

Recipes
Featuring First Fruits Of The Land

Let me share some period recipes with you as a perfect topping to a chapter on fruit.

Real Apple Cider Vinegar

Nothing like the stuff you buy, this is fruity and delicate. Great for a little extra pizzazz in stir frys, steamed vegetables, soups, salad dressings, or roasted meats.

1/2 gallon raw, unpasturized apple cider

1 pint real, unpasturized apple cider vinegar (usually found at health food stores)

Mix into 1 gallon plastic or glass container. Put the lid on loosely and wait about 30–45 days. A surface film may form. This is normal, just skim off before use. (It's the wild yeast, also called the "mother.") You can also let raw cider sit and let nature take its course, but you may end up with "hard" cider instead of vinegar—a treat in its own right.

Switchel

Health and frugality often went hand-in-hand in earlier days. An interesting taste from the past can be recreated by preparing this traditional drink from real apple cider vinegar. Crisp and light, it was carried by children out to the field hands during harvest. Interestingly, recent research points to the health benefits of raw vinegar in the diet.

1 gallon spring water

1–2 c. cider vinegar

1–2 c. brown sugar

fresh grated ginger to taste

1 cup unsulfered molasses or low grade maple syrup

Warm water to dissolve sugar and molasses

Add vinegar and ginger. Cool in glass or crockery container. Serve chilled.

CIDER—A DRINK FROM THE PAST

Rare is the person nowadays who has had the privilege of drinking real, "hard" cider. Freshly pressed, unpasturized juice often carries the label "cider," but until allowed to ferment into a clear, clean wine it isn't truly cider.

Several old varieties of cider trees are now extinct, many destroyed intentionally as part of the Works Progress Administration during the depression. It was thought by destroying these heirloom trees, disease and insect problems of modern orchards would be reduced.

Fortunately, there were survivors including; Baldwin, McIntosh, Red and Roxberry Russet. Since good apples are the heart and soul of good cider, a blend of tart, sweet, and neutral makes for the best flavor.

The pulp leftover from pressing (pomace) was buried in pits around orchards to control apple maggots, effectively trapping them. It was also used as livestock feed, fertilizer and weed killer (due to its acidic nature).

It's also a terrific additive to the compost heap.

For a real trip into history, Wassail or toast each of your fruit trees in January with a cup of cider to encourage fruiting.

So plant some trees, rent a press and enjoy the good life with some real cider.

FIVE

EMIGRANT MEMORIES

Their Favorite Flowers

ONE OF THE MOST IMPORTANT REASONS settlers gardened, especially the women, was for remembering. They didn't refer to themselves as pioneers but rather as emigrants. They had left the United States and all they had known for a wild and uncertain future. While the men made a journey of hope, the women were often reluctant followers. Strangers in a strange land, these women made the journey out of loyalty to their husbands. They were the ones who would push to build schools, churches, and libraries. They were the ones who would "civilize" the country by maintaining beauty and tradition, each in her own way. The seeds and plants from home were very important symbols of their past. Until the advent of seed catalogs and nurseries, plants were passed from generation to generation. A bride's dowry commonly contained seeds to start her own garden as a new wife.

HATCHET HANDS

HOE

MADAM PLANTIER ROSE

One of the early settlers in the Portland area made flowers her special community work. After her land on the Mount Tabor claim was cleared, one of the first things she did was plant white flowers. Where panthers still screamed in the night, she tended her garden, sharing her flowers with her neighbors.

Community gatherings were so very important. Weddings, dances, and the like were an opportunity to share food, music, and flowers. More often, though, there were

funerals—especially among the children. The formal rites of "laying away" the beloved provided families great comfort. It was a strong sentiment among the settlers that the best they had must be for their dead. White was the traditional color for flowers at funerals and in the early days it must have been quite a work to supply the

LILIUM WALLICHIANUM

VINCA GROWING AT KEIL CEMETERY

demand. Later, as the area became more settled, this Mount Tabor settler was able to share her flowers for more joyous occasions. Many years later, as a very old woman on her own death bed, her mind wandered to her garden, her last words being of all her beautiful white flowers.

Cemeteries were filled with favorite flowers. Planted around and atop of the graves, each family's story was told. Snowdrops, thyme, lunaria, narcissus, violets, and a host of others sweetened these sad places. Vinca, or the purple peri-

How To Know The Wild Flowers

CANADA VIOLET

ROSE DECORATES GRAVE AT LONE FIR CEMETERY

winkle, was especially common and can be found in abundance around many old cemeteries. It has the happy property of growing in shade and poor soil, making it ideal for gravesites. Aside from practical considerations, the periwinkle was considered a "flower of mystery." The French referred to it as the "Violette des Sorciers" and in Tuscany it was called the "Flower of Death," used as garlands at the burials of children. The British folk name was joy-of-the-ground.

How To Know The Wild Flowers

NIGHTSHADE

Nightshade was another of the "plants of mystery" found around gravesites, often climbing up an old oak tree. Its connotations of truth and death are best summed up in its alternate name, Bittersweet.

These strong European traditions exerted a lasting influence on the pioneers where families passed on the old ways generation after

LILAC OVER CHILD'S GRAVE, CANEMAH CEMETERY

generation. Sadly, in the name of progress, this custom of planting flowers on graves has been abandoned in favor of the uniformity and order of mechanized maintenance. Still, hardy survivors persist—especially in less groomed cemeteries where pockets of white violets, grape hyacinths, yellow daffodils (called butter and eggs), periwinkle, and perennial sweet peas can still be found underfoot.

Farm Festivals

CHILDREN PLACING FLOWERS AT GRAVE OF A LOVED ONE

In a Molalla, Oregon pioneer cemetery, a dozen or more varieties of old roses, brought and planted by early families, adorned the graves until the cemetery was taken over by the city in the 1980s. For convenience, all the old roses were destroyed. But, blessedly, a pioneer descendent living nearby had the foresight to take cuttings, and maintains them in her own garden.

DIANTHUS CRUENTUS

The large trees and shrubs we associate with cemeteries are the remnants of these old plantings, each having special meanings. Holly (the blood of Christ); Yucca (eternal life); Yew (sorrow); Lilac, which was very often planted over children's graves (sentiment and youth); Camellia (perfected loveliness); Oaks and Cedars (strength and permanence).

In thinking of plants the pioneers brought, most probably expect romantic

Courtesy Clackamas County Historical Society

TWO UNIDENTIFIED DANDIES
Perhaps they are collecting wildflowers for their sweethearts.

things like ivy and roses, which were certainly popular, but the pioneers also brought Christmas cactus and iceplant. These were not faceless, uniform people. They were as different as you and I. One gentleman, a pastor in the Oregon goldfields, planted a large flower garden in the middle of nowhere. He complained of the summer frosts that damaged his more tender flowers, yet enough survived that he had a constant stream of women and children visiting. They would make a day's journey by foot just to see his garden. The children would beg for handfuls of "pretties" to take home to their mothers.

Ladies lucky enough to have their own flowers, would plant them right by the kitchen door—boxed by packing crates to fend off roving chickens. There they flourished, nurtured by the bountiful wash water from the cabin. Gardeners today may love their flowers, but in that time they were also a hope of softer times to come. Mrs. Matheney, an early settler, came well prepared to plant her garden. Placing all her seeds in a bag, she carried them over the trail wrapped around her saddle horn. Riding most of the way, she was able to protect her treasures from the dangers of the wagon—especially in river crossings. Her hungry family complained of her "stinginess" about her seeds while on the trail. Only once did she unwrap a few peas to cook at a most desperate time. Later, her daughter would recall how glad she was that Mother had been so protective. Not only did they have a fine vegetable garden, but Mrs. Matheney also had the first real flower garden in the valley: a wonder to all who passed. Her special pride were her pinks (dianthus) that she bred almost to the perfection of modern day carnations.

Peonies were a very popular plant in those days. One particular peony has a very interesting story. Dr. Keil was the founder of a society based on communal living. He and his followers decided to leave for the new lands of the West to establish a brand new town based on their religious beliefs.

They were certain this new place would become heaven on earth but just before leaving Dr. Keil's son, Willie, became very ill. Knowing he would soon die, Willie begged his father not to leave him behind. Dr. Keil gave his word that he would not. When Willie died, his body was placed in a lead-lined casket filled with whiskey. A special wagon was commissioned

FLORAL MEANINGS FROM
AMANDA MANN'S REMEMBRANCE BOOK, 1865

Foxglove...I am not ambitious for myself but for you
Lunaria...Wish not for perishable riches
Columbine...I will not give thee up
Rose...May you taste the sweets of true friendship
Snow Ball...Virtues cluster around thee
Tulip...Vanity
Chamomile...Cheerfulness in adversity

Sweet William...One may smile and be a villain still
Honeysuckle....Bonds of love
White Lily...Purity
Yellow Rose Bud....Deceive me once your fault, twice mine
Sweet Pea...Must we part?
Peach...Here I fix my choice
Campanula....Gratitude
Scotch Broom...How I am bereaved
Locust...Affection beyond the grave
Peony....Ostentation

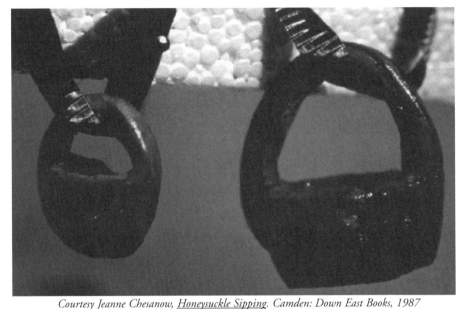

Courtesy Jeanne Chesanow, <u>Honeysuckle Sipping</u>. Camden: Down East Books, 1987

NUT BASKETS
A simple craft for pioneer children.

FLOWER FUN

Sipping nectar from flowers like fuch-sias and honeysuckle was a favorite summer past-time. Dolls made of flow-ers were fashioned from all kinds of flora.

Hollyhocks were favorite subjects, their huge flowers making billowing dresses when turned over. They can even be made to "dance" by twirling them in a pan of water.

so Willie's remains could make the trip to the promised land for burial.

Throughout the crossing, Indians visited the train. But it wasn't to make trouble. The natives just wanted to see the traveling body that was the talk of the trail! Dr. Keil's people arrived safely, as did a peony brought on that same wagon train.

While Dr. Keil buried his dead son, this family planted a peony as living testament to their heritage. When the family left the Aurora colony, the peony went with them and has been moved three or so times since. That original plant, from the Keil colony, lives today in Monmouth, Oregon, a survivor of more than one hundred and fifty years.

The Leach Family also settled near Aurora in 1847. Their grandson, John, married Lilla in the family pasture where a moss-covered tree stump served as an altar. When the family farm was sold, John sawed off the stump and moved it to their new garden. There Lilla planted a matrimony vine over it.

Flowers for remembrance was a favorite Victorian theme, especially among young girls. Kate Greenway's book *The Language Of Flowers* was in every household bookshelf. She resurrected the traditions of the middle ages when every plant was assigned a meaning. A bouquet was actually a letter, in a

LILAC PLAY

Girls would make garlands of lilacs by tucking individual flower heads together into long chains. Sometimes special lilacs having five divisions, instead of the normal four, would be found.

These were called "luck" lilacs. When swallowed, if it went down smoothly the girl would say "He loves me;" if she choked she had to say "He loves me not."

PHILLIP FOSTER FARM AND LILAC IN WINTER

time when very few were literate. For the Victorians, it was a part of a great movement, returning to romance and nature.

The archives at Marylhurst have a beautiful remembrance book. It belonged to Amanda Mann, the first graduate of St. Mary's Academy. Dated 1865, there are pressed flowers, wild and cultivated, with their Latin names and their meaning in the language of flowers. The calligraphy and handwriting are works of art. This book has so rarely been opened that many of the flowers still retain their color.

Lilacs were a favorite shrub favored for their sweet, May fragrance. Mrs. Foster (Phillip's wife) brought a lilac from New England around the Horn by ship. Planted at the Foster Farm, that old lilac has bloomed continually since it was planted. The local historical society has a special Mother's Day sale each year where they sell starts of the lilac to help support the Foster Farm. Lilacs were also planted as hedges, although the rust fungus has made most of these a style in memory only.

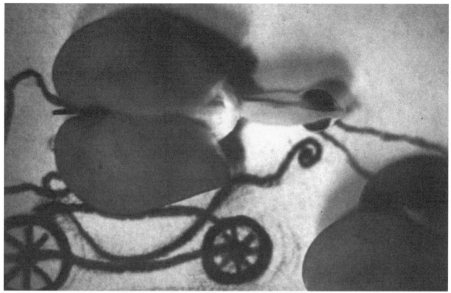

Courtesy Jeanne Chesanow, <u>Honeysuckle Sipping</u>. Camden: Down East Books, 1987

BLEEDING HEART CINDERELLA'S COACH

LADY-IN-THE-BOAT BLEEDING HEARTS

Courtesy Jeanne Chesanow, <u>Honeysuckle Sipping</u>. Camden: Down East Books, 1987

From <u>Fanny</u>, by permission of Joyce Badgley Hunsaker, Tom Novak, Illustrator

FANNY AND HER HOLLYHOCK SEEDS

One of the most beloved flowers of the emigrants were the single pink hollyhocks. Joyce Hunsaker, a pioneer descendent, has created a living history character named "Fanny" based on the diaries of pioneer women. Much of the material comes from her own great-grandmother's journey across the Oregon Trail. Here is one of Fanny's stories.

It was the day they were to leave. Everywhere was noise and confusion. Wagons; pink, red, and green jockeying for position. Fanny nervously sits in the wagon, peering through the dust, praying that her mother will come. She had been too busy the night before to say good-bye. Finally, there, running through the crowd, Fanny sees her mamma. Breathless, Mamma places her hand on the wagon and, looking up at Fanny tells her, "Fanny girl, I don't know if I shall ever again see you in this life." Then Mamma opens Fanny's hand, placing a kerchief tied at the corners in it. Without another word, she turns her back on Fanny and the wagons begin to roll. Fanny is just in shock, why didn't Mamma look back? As the tears roll down her face she remembers the kerchief in her hand. What could have been so important that Mamma would have left this as a last gift for her daughter? Fanny unties the kerchief and there, in her hand, are the seeds of the

The American West in the Nineteenth Century

NIGHTTIME ON THE TRAIL
Horses were driven into a corral formed by the wagons to keep them from running off or being stolen by Indians. The drawing by Theodore R. Davis was first pictured in *Harper's Weekly*, June 12, 1869.

single, pink hollyhock that Mama had always grown by the front door. Fanny puts the kerchief away and tells us of her experiences on the trail, including the death of her young daughter. At the end, she takes out her kerchief and tells us that she will "plant these seeds year, after year, after year because she has survived year, after year, after year." And she did. Through all those generations, the family planted those seeds and shared the stories uniting their family across the miles and years. That's living history!

It doesn't matter if you're a pioneer descendent, it matters that you remember and share that courage and determination with others. It is hope that allows folks to endure their own tough times. What better hope can there be than remembering those who have gone before us and survived?

The American West in the Nineteenth Century

NEWLY-ARRIVED PIONEER FAMILY
The Frenzeny and Tavernier drawing of frontier home-building first appeared in *Harper's Weekly*, January 24, 1874.

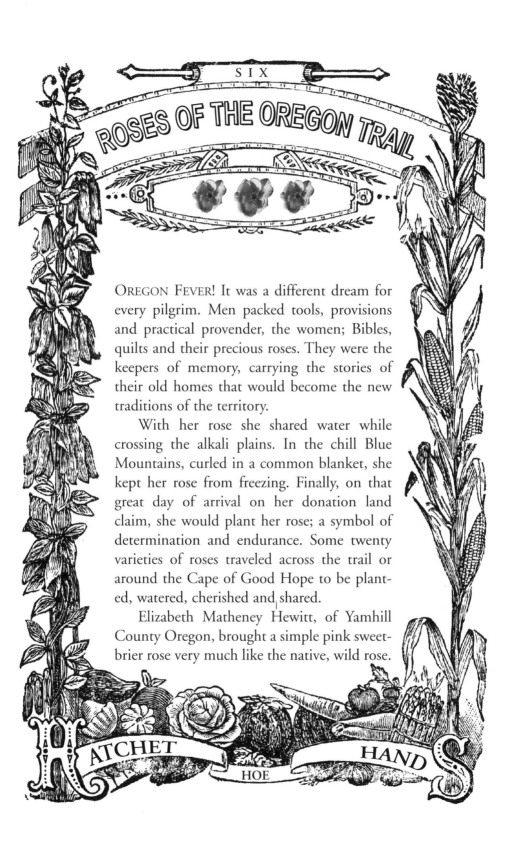

SIX

ROSES OF THE OREGON TRAIL

OREGON FEVER! It was a different dream for every pilgrim. Men packed tools, provisions and practical provender, the women; Bibles, quilts and their precious roses. They were the keepers of memory, carrying the stories of their old homes that would become the new traditions of the territory.

With her rose she shared water while crossing the alkali plains. In the chill Blue Mountains, curled in a common blanket, she kept her rose from freezing. Finally, on that great day of arrival on her donation land claim, she would plant her rose; a symbol of determination and endurance. Some twenty varieties of roses traveled across the trail or around the Cape of Good Hope to be plant-ed, watered, cherished and shared.

Elizabeth Matheney Hewitt, of Yamhill County Oregon, brought a simple pink sweet-brier rose very much like the native, wild rose.

HATCHET HANDS

HOE

'DEAD' LATIN
LANGUAGE OF LIVE PLANTS

Rugosa — *wrinkled*

Gallica — *from France, also refers to rooster*

Multiflora — *many flowered*

Centifolia — *many petaled*

Rubinagosa — *rust, ruddy, red*

Alba — *white or pale colored*

Glauca — *bluish gray*

Setigera — *bristle bearing*

Officinalis — *medicinal, of the pharmacopoeia or apothecary*

Damask — *of Damascus, Syria*

Discovering the Origins, Lore and Meanings of Botanical Names

It did so well that one of the family men quietly complained, as he grubbed it out of a field; "I wish Elizabeth hadn't done that." Ironically, a couple generations later when this man's grave was visited by his family, it was nearly smothered by Elizabeth's sweetbrier.

The Matheneys settled near the site of the old Lee Mission. Although the mission burned in the early 1840s, some of the plantings of the missionaries survived. One of the missionaries, Mrs. Beers, sailed from Boston in 1836 with a party of Methodists to settle near Champoeg, Oregon.

With her came a start of a rose. The long voyage was extended more than six weeks when ill winds detained the ship before at last rounding the Cape. The delay threatened the water supply of the ship to the point where the ladies each

Courtesy Oregon Historical Society

JASON LEE'S MISSION, SALEM, OREGON

gave a share of their drinking water to support the withered slip. Mrs. Beers presented the rose as a wedding gift to Anna Marie Pitman, Jason Lee's bride. Sadly, Anna never got to see the rose bloom, she died in childbirth the following June. It became tradition, even with this first unfortunate precedent, for brides married in the Valley to get a start of this "Mission Rose." The original plant was left to the wilds when the mission was abandoned where John Minto rediscovered it in a field and planted it on his claim. He also shared it with the Matheney family where it held a prized spot in Elizabeth's garden. Since they operated a ferry, the Matheney's had many visitors and the rose was shared with all who asked. Strangely, this famous rose has become the source of much confusion. Several different varieties have claimed the honored title of *The* Mission Rose, a tangle that still needs resolving. Adding to the confusion, the garden at Fort Vancouver also had a "mission rose" but it may be an entirely different plant with its origins in the Spanish Missions of California. One family of hop growers had an interesting tradition about roses.

The patriarch of the clan would always plant a rose at the end of every hop row. When asked why he simply replied that there should always be "beauty in the field."

The sweetbrier was favored by many families. A tall, lanky plant with simple, pink flowers its special beauty is in the fresh, sweet scent of its leaves. Once smelled, particularly after a rain, her perfume is never forgotten.

Children enjoyed eating the fresh shoots in the spring as a special treat, likening the flavor to bubble gum. The sweetbrier will happily grow up trees and thrive in partial shade, a real plus in Northwest gardens. The Denney family, instrumental in the settlement of Seattle, is also famous for their "sweetbrier bride." Miss Louisa Boren was almost a spinster by the standards of the time, in her mid-twenties when she married Mr. Denny, who was a scandalous few years her junior.

They met and fell in love as they traveled together on the wagon train. Her treasure were the seeds of a sweetbrier taken from home. Splitting them with her best friend, each pledged to plant their seeds by the door of their homes; one in the old land and one in the new; a living token of their friendship.

ROSE "TOBACCO"

Mainly a child's treat, this was a special gift between friends. In a glass jar, layer rose petals with brown sugar. Fragrant, old roses work best. Don't use any roses that have been treated with chemicals, especially systemic compounds. Allow to stand 2–3 weeks. This rose flavored sugar makes a great candy or a moist potpourri. Try some in an herb tea for a real old fashioned flavor. (You can also do this with violets).

After many trials, the sweetbrier bloomed in the new land but, ironically in the relative safety of civilization, Mrs. Denney's girlhood friend died before she could plant hers. Mrs. Denney was known in early Seattle for her extravagant flower gardens, fulfilling her promise to her friend even in death.

Harrison's Yellow, also known as the Governor's Seal, can be found the length of the Oregon Trail. It thrives particularly in the drier regions where huge thickets mark the spots of long lost homesteads. Discovered accidentally in New York in the 1830s, its disease and drought resistance made it a favorite of travelers. A wonderful poem by Florence Kerr, published in the *Oregonian* February 15, 1981 captures this lasting affection for Harrison's Yellow.

A THOUSAND MEMORIES

With a lilac shoot and a yellow rose root
hidden under the seat of the wagon;
and with hollyhock seeds and a day lily corm
tied into the corner of a flour bag towel,
Great-Grandmother first came West.

Close to the cabin she planted the hoard,
watered them with the dishwater,
fearlessly waved her ruffled petticoats to fright-
en off the roaming cattle;
and so it was, her treasures multiplied.

Today I tend the lovely rose;
along my fence the hollyhocks grow tall.
No flower shows would grant them ribbons,
but this much I would have you share:
For me, they hold a thousand memories.

Courtesy Pacific University Archivess

MARY DRAIN ALBRO
Standing second from the left, Albro and other dignitaries dedicate the
pioneer rose garden and women's monument, June 4, 1949.

In the late 1920s a pioneer descendent, Mary Drain Albro,
set out to find and rescue the surviving Oregon Trail roses.
Born in 1876, Mrs. Albro's preservation work was particularly important since she had first hand accounts from pioneer
families.

On one expedition, Mrs. Albro retrieved a root of an old
rose from a dilapidated arbor. Disturbed by her grubbing, a
pile of tiny piglets began enthusiastic squealing. A moment
later, Mrs. Albro heard a far more threatening sound—the
grunts of a very angry mother sow headed her way. With rose
in one hand and mattock in the other, she jumped the the old
stone fence to escape, never letting go of either rose or mattock. Fifty–plus years old at the time, it must have been quite
a scene.

Mrs. Albro established the Pioneer Rose Society and over the years established gardens at Champoeg, Pacific University at Forest Grove, and Portland's Lone Fir Cemetery.

By the time of Mrs. Albro's death in 1962, much of her work was already vanishing. Today, sadly, only a portion of the Lone Fir collection remains. These "old ladies," living survivors of the Oregon Trail, have some wonderful stories to tell. Like any grandmother, they appreciate a chance to share their memories.

Surveying techniques were a bit lacking when the early emigrants took up their claims. Later generations often contested the boundaries bitterly. A no-mans-land, called a "mad lane" often resulted. One family involved in a particularly difficult dispute was bemoaning the situation to their grandmother, the original settler on the claim. The old lady patiently listened and then smiled as she took the family out to the "mad lane."

In the growth of brambles, she pointed out a row of old roses, nearly smothered by the blackberries, planted long ago by her to mark the property line. As the story spread throughout the valley,

ROSE RUSTLING

Gardeners in Texas coined this phrase when they began to go forth by bands to preserve their living history. Old roses are most commonly found in cemeteries, abandoned homesites or neglected old homes. Always go with a friend (just in case you meet a mad sow) and try to get permission first.

The cardinal rule in collecting is never to take the entire plant unless it is threatened. A rooted piece of rose has the best chance of success although a cutting near a dormant bud will work for some roses.

Dip your root or slip in rooting hormone or make your own by soaking willow twigs in water. If you use willow water, let the rose start sit in it overnight.

Start your rose in a light soil mixed with compost in a pot. Leave in a protected, semi-shady area until it's really going, then plant out in your garden and enjoy.

The Beginner's Reader

the Old Cardinal also became known as the "Witness Rose." Grown by General Lane, late 1870s.

By a nameless riverside, a young mother gently cradles her dying daughter. The year is 1852 on the Oregon Trail and cholera has almost claimed another victim. Softly smoothing her child's hair with water, the mother baptizes her girl before burial. A boy, four or so, looks on and finally questions, "Mamma, why are you putting water on little sister?"

Quietly, the young woman replies "We're getting ready to give her to God for an angel."

In the morning, the wagons roll on leaving another small grave in their wake. Months later, finally arrived in the new land the same mother, plants a slip of a rose brought from home—her little piece of beauty and hope. While watering the slip her son trots by and asks "Mamma are you giving that rose to God for an angel too?" *(See Color Plate I).*

Strangely, Mrs. Albro never mentioned the rose brought by her own family across the plains. The yellow Father Hugo rose was planted at the Drain mansion in Drain, Oregon and cuttings of this rose can be found throughout Douglas County. Another "mystery" rose that even Mrs. Albro wasn't able to ferret out, was the Lost Plate rose. In an interview with an aged lady, Mrs. Albro confirmed its existence in pioneer times. The size of a small dinner plate, this rose had single, purple-red flowers and was a favorite among the children.

The climate of the Willamette Valley was apparently not to its liking and since it wasn't a very attractive rose (at least in the eyes of grown-ups) it was allowed to die out.

Old roses and cemeteries certainly go together. Many have survived through benign neglect in pioneer cemeteries. A very special piece of living history has been preserved in Oregon City's historic Mountain View Cemetery.

The Hunsaker family had been one of the earliest families to emigrate. They had done so well, they wrote home to encourage the rest of the clan to come west. In 1852 the rest of the Hunsakers, including their daughter Josephine, arrived in Oregon City. Josephine was one of those blessed children that everyone loved. Even her brothers and sisters looked on her as more of a mother than a sister. Being Catholic, they sent Josephine to a school run by nuns near Fort Vancouver. By early winter Josephine had returned home but there was to be no celebrating. The entire family, excepting the father, came down with typhoid or mountain fever, as it was sometimes called. Dr. McLoughlin, hearing of their plight, came down from Fort Vancouver to personally render assistance. Being Catholic

HARDY TREE ROSES
Advertised in an early-day gardening catalog: "Price, $2.00 each or two for $3.50."

JOSEPHINE'S GRAVE

himself, he was well acquainted with the family and brought with him a special gift for Josephine; a cutting of a rose from his personal garden. He hoped it would speed her recovery by cheering her but sadly, both she and her brother Horton died in the spring.

They were buried together where the grieving mother planted a slip of the rose behind their grave. Unfortunately,

RUBBING OF JOSEPHINE'S
HEADSTONE

the story was lost for many years and the rose was mowed down each May, ironically to tidy the cemetery for Memorial Day.

Nearly dead, this historic rose was rescued by Nancy Wilson, curator of the McLoughlin House. Thanks to her nurturing care, its sweet damask scent can now be enjoyed each spring and autumn. The story is bitter-sweet but the real message is how important it is for each of us to be the keepers of memory for our communities and our families; to take the extra time to share a little water and a little room in our gardens for these old plants that have such stories to share.

The creed of the Pioneer Rose Association captures the love and sentimentality folks of earlier days had for their roses. It's also a perfect tribute to all the settlers who planted the pioneer spirit in their gardens and a call to us to continue their work.

AN OLD ROSE AT THE GATE

To us it had traveled long miles o'er the plain,
To bloom in the sun and drink in the rain
When the lark in the meadow would fly up to sing,
With fresh, happy tidings, "Dear child, it is spring".

Then Grandmother dear would plan for her store,
No matter if plenty, she always had more.
When strangers would pause to rest for the night,
To warm by the fire and sip by the light,
To sing the old hymn, then kneel down to pray
A custom they lived in Pioneer Day.

Gone is the day and gone is the door,
Where the stranger once paused to take of her store,
But ours is the day when the Roses bloom free
Again in the land for you and for me.
From homestead and grave, by highway and field,
We gathered the Rose of pioneer yield,
In story of her we remember so well,
With the home and the grave for Roses to tell
To drink in the rain and bloom in the spring,
When once more the lark will fly up to sing.

When the stranger will pause to sip and to ask
We'll tell of our love and the joy of the task,
Of the hymn and the prayer when evening grew late
And the Pioneer Rose at Grandmother's gate.

OLD ROSES GRACE A PRESENT-DAY GATE
The Pioneer Spirit Lives On.

BUNGALOW WITH ROCK GARDEN

APPENDIX

Garden Recreations:
The Rest of the Story

OWNERS OF OLD HOMES don't need to be sold on the joy and importance of using their living space to preserve the past. Homes, lovingly restored down to the finest detail, convey not only an architectural era, but personal stories of past and present owners as well.

Unfortunately, landscaping usually falls at the end of a project when finances, energy and enthusiasm are at an ebb. The landscape should be as important an architectural accent as the proper hardware. Casual inspection of many wonderful, old homes reveal unimaginative lawns, barkdust and shrubbery. Alice Morris Earl, a garden writer from the 1920s, wrote that the desire for lawn was the enemy of the garden. Historic gardening is certainly an appropriate homeowner project. With patience, you can achieve both accuracy and economy.

A garden will usually require a recreation versus a restoration. Living materials are perishable. A few years neglect or an owner who wants to reduce the maintenance and the garden is gone. Surviving trees and shrubs may provide a skeleton of the old landscape but the "flesh and blood," the flowering plants, are usually only a distant memory.

CONTAINER GARDEN LINES BUNGALOW PORCH AND WALK

Most folks will want to create an heirloom garden versus a truly historic renovation. An heirloom garden uses plants appropriate to a period planted in a basically traditional style. Plants similar in appearance to their ancestors may be substituted if originals can't be obtained. An heirloom garden allows more freedom of expression and can be more practical to install. A true historic garden is for those who need to landscape museums or other important historical sites.

STEP 1: INVENTORY

The first step is a cautious inventory of the existing landscape. This will require patience as it should be conducted over a year's time. Help from a garden consultant or landscaper might be helpful here, particularly if the space is very overgrown. It will be important to identify key features for preservation like old fruit trees and lilacs. Many plants will need to be pruned or removed but knowing which are significant can help you plan. Clearing away surplus vegetation; grass, ivy etc. will help you do a better inventory.

Some old plants look very different from their modern cousins (another reason it is good to get some help in identification during the inventory). An acquaintance of mine in our local "Old Home Forum" graciously shared her experience. She has a fabulous garden that has been featured in magazines more than once.

When she first moved into her old home there was little remaining except some old moss roses. The buds of the roses are surrounded by sticky, hairy (mossy) sepals. They have a fresh, piney fragrance that was highly prized in Victorian times. To my friend's modern eyes, however, these mossy buds appeared diseased. She dug them all out, destroying the last remnants of her old garden. *(See Color Plate K)*.

Patience comes into play particularly when considering the unseen. Many wonderful old perennials like; peonies, iris and daffodils lay dormant most of the year. Installing a major landscape project before an inventory could destroy these old plants before the homeowner is even aware of their existence.

When we moved into our 1910 farmhouse in Oregon City, it was May. Grass was shin high in the yard and waist high in the fields. Comfrey, lemon balm, and lunaria ran rampant. Clearly, maintenance was long overdue. Setting to work, it took two steady, sweaty weeks to prune, weed, thin, and mow. Four months pregnant, in the middle of the hottest summer on record, thoughts of preserving hidden botanical treasures were far from my mind. Like the pioneers my mind was set on subduing this untamed land.

By summer's end, I had established several heirloom gardens including a rose, herb, and vegetable garden. I was victorious—or so I thought.

After a long winter, spring arrived and, to my delight, hundreds of spring bulbs magically appeared. An additional coup was the unfolding of a rare plant—the majestic Maija

SENATOR JONES HOME IN AN HISTORIC PHOTOGRAPH
The house is located in Oregon City, Oregon.

Poppy (Romnea Coulterii). Chagrined, I realized how easily these old stands could have been lost through my carelessness.

Our second season brought us the joys of septic repair. After divining the tank location, I was horrified to discover it lay under the edge of my dooryard (herb garden).

The moral of the story is: consideration of the unseen in gardening doesn't only relate to plants. As we continue to garden (with a somewhat looser hand) old perennials continue to appear and multiply—apparently happy with their new keepers. Perseverance does pay. Negative examples, although embarrassing, serve to point out the importance of care in the early stages of planning. Hopefully, they also offer encouragement to those who feel they face an impossible task and wonder if they're doing the right thing.

STEP 2: EVALUATION

In laying out a plan, work as much as possible with existing structures, landforms and key vegetation. Taking a less intru-

SENATOR JONES HOUSE TODAY

sive approach not only reduces costs but may also reveal the hidden garden that once existed. The 1913 Senator Jones House in Oregon City is an example of this kind of happy coincidence.

In 1989 when the garden was begun, only an overgrown wisteria and steep thatchy lawn remained. The owner, Cathie Daniels, first tried a vegetable garden—only to discover that passersby kept pilfering it (another planning consideration).

As they leveled the yard, stone after stone was uncovered. Like New England farmers, the Daniels' stacked them into a series of low walls. Planting simple, hardy plants here and there, a pocket of beauty was created on this semi–commercial street: a tapestry of old fashioned perennials.

Later, while doing additional research on the house, Cathie recovered a turn-of-the-century photo of their home. Thrilled, she realized that the garden in the photo looked very similar to the one she had created.

I experienced a similar thrill when all my old garden gems poked up in the very "rooms" I had created: a stamp of approval from flower lovers, now long gone. The sense of working beside another gardener from a century before is indescribably fulfilling.

STEP 3: RESEARCH

Once you have a basic idea of where you want to plant and, perhaps some idea of style, the next step is to do the research to flesh it out. Your choice of heirloom or true historic recreation will dictate the depth of digging you need to do. It may be possible to hire a consultant to guide you but frankly, if you have the time, this is one of the most rewarding and interesting aspects of garden planning. Aside from the botanical information you will gather, you will also get a peek at the daily life of the era you're investigating.

Archival Photos: These will be one of your best resources. Although individual plants will be difficult to identify, it will give you a sense of style. If the images are clear enough, you can have copies made and a consultant can work with you in identification. These photos are most often found in museums, university collections and, occasionally libraries. Begin with the obvious categories, such as gardens, flowers, and agriculture. Photographs from state and county fairs can also be helpful as winners of prize produce or flowers are often pictured. Categories covering architecture and schools often depict exterior views as do family collections. Be forewarned, however, it is very easy to get pleasantly distracted sorting through hundreds of old photographs if you're any kind of a nostalgia buff.

I have been fortunate in finding many old garden photos in family collections, as they seemed to be a favorite backdrop for portraits. You can save money by Xeroxing the photos if you only need basic information, instead of having prints made. Just be certain to put any available information on the reverse before you leave the resource site. I guarantee you will forget if you don't.

The Written Word: Garden columns in old newspapers and magazines are a great resource as are local extension records. Oral history transcripts can be very helpful, although you'll need a lot of patience to get the garden gleanings from them. Homemakers and homesteaders were favorite sources for these oral histories and their first hand accounts often provide varietal as well as cultural information. One of the absolute best sources are period catalogs. These are often found co-located with archival photographs. The lists and illustrations are invaluable but they can really make you long for the prices from the past.

If you're in a time crunch, hire a researcher or do your investigations by phone. Call, fax, or write your research facilities with your requests. Examine leads by fax or post then have selected materials sent to you. The staff researchers will charge for their time and, unless they have a focus on your subject, you may not get all you hope for.

Doing your research in person can often lead to unexpected treasures. I was privileged to find an 1865, *Victorian Remembrance Book* filled with pressed flowers. Many retained their color and all were identified by genus and species with artistic calligraphy. Not only did I have a document that listed period plants, but a gem of great beauty to record.

STEP 4: PRODUCING THE PLAN

I won't go into a detailed account of landscape planning, there are many fine books and professionals to guide you here. Try (I know, I don't do it either—but try) to bite off one area at a time and develop it fully. Have a basic plant list, developed from previous steps, and some period plant associations before you begin sketching off your garden "rooms." A basic checklist will cover items such as:

Money: What is your initial budget and long range maintenance budget?

Who: Will you do the work or hire it out? (Consider time and skills needed)

Methods: Will you install or maintain the garden using historic methods?

Restrictions: Is there zoning or covenant restrictions that limit your plan?

Use: How will you use your garden? Food?, Cut flowers? Entertainment?

Lifestyle: What times of day will you be in the garden? Do you have children or pets?

Views: Consider your garden from the inside out. Create views you'll enjoy year round from the inside. Think about how they will change by time of day and season.

The list goes on and on. This is just to get you started thinking about the details. Remember, gardening is not a static art form. You—and it—will change over time. Blessedly, most heirloom plants are amazingly forgiving. You'll learn from both your successes and your failures, so be bold and dig in!

GARDEN BORDER BEAUTIFIES THE FRONT OF THIS HOUSE

STEP 5: GETTING THE PROPER PLANTS

There are many advantages of using heirloom plants in the landscape. Most are easy to propagate and once established need a minimum of care. Their hardy nature is the very reason they are still with us today. Just don't confuse *low* maintenance with *no* maintenance.

Aside from buying from a nursery or landscaper you may want,or need, some additional plant sources.

Seeds: Fortunately, as the interest in heirloom gardening grows more and more small seed companies and historic sites are offering heirloom seeds. Local garden clubs, Master Gardeners and, especially, the Seed Savers Exchange can also be excellent sources. *Warning:* Many seed companies offering old varieties are honest and ethical but some are not. They may offer an old variety by name that is actually completely different when planted out. The maze of ensuring that a plant is genetically identical to one grown long ago is incredibly

PIONEER GARDEN RECREATION
The site is the historic Philip Foster Farm is in Eagle Creek, Oregon.

complex. Name changes, regional adaptations etc. make seed purity an exacting art.

"Rustling:" If you are fortunate enough to live in an area of old homes and cemeteries you may be able to salvage some wonderful old plants by "rustling". There are groups throughout the US that take cuttings or divisions of old plants in order to preserve and enjoy them. Legitimate groups always get permission and never take an entire plant unless it is threatened. Rose enthusiasts led the charge but as the practice grows, you might join a band of "perennial pinchers." Aside from the plants you obtain, you'll gain valuable skills in identification, propagation and culture.

A caution: If you choose the rigorous course of restoring a historical garden, proceed with caution. I have been given a number of plants that claim their origins in pioneer gardens. I value them highly and have them in a special border until I can do more research on them. Documenting on the basis of hearsay is a recipe for disappointment down the line. If you are doing research at a historical garden, try to track down their original research, take nothing for granted.

Our gardens can not only provide accurate, architectural accents for our old homes but can also assist preservation efforts in world of shrinking biological diversity. Perhaps more importantly, they can tell the stories of an era, a community, or a family: a continuity Lincoln called "the mystic cords of memory." Cords that provide the framework for weaving a more livable future.

PLANT SOURCES

Obviously this is only a partial list, there are many small local nurseries that offer great plants but we include these folks because we know them—and they're great.

Territorial Seed Company
PO Box 157
Cottage Grove, OR 97424

Nicols Garden Nursery, Inc.
1190 N. Pacific Hwy.
Albany, OR 97321

Raintree Nursery
391 Butts Rd.
Morton, WA 98356

Logee's Greenhouses
141 North Street
Danielson, CT 06239

Select Seeds
10080 Stickney Hill Rd.
Union, CT 06076

Ronnigers Seed Potatoes
Star Route
Moyie Springs, ID 83845

Caprice Nursery (Daylilies, peonies, and iris)
15425 SW Pleasant Hill Rd.
Sherwood, OR 97140

Heirloom Old Garden Roses
24062 NE Riverside Drive
St. Paul, OR 97137

Fox Hollow Herb & Heirloom Seed Co.
PO Box 148
Mc Grann, PA 16236

Heirloom Seeds
PO Box 245
W. Elizabeth, PA 15088

Filaree Farms (Garlic)
Route 1 Box 162
Okanogan, WA 98840

Old House Gardens (Bulbs)
536 Third St.
Ann Arbor, MI 48103

Johnny's Selected Seeds
Foss Hill Rd.
Albion, ME 04910

ORGANIZATIONS, NEWSLETTERS, & RESOURCES

Seed Savers Exchange
3076 N. Winn Rd.
Decorah, IA 52101

Niggletytwist Historic Gardening
15301 S. Loder Rd.
Oregon City, OR 97045

The Historical Gardener
1910 N. 35th Pl.
Mt. Vernon, WA 98273

The Thomas Jefferson Center for Historic Plants
Monticello PO Box 316
Charlottesville, VA 22902

The Home Orchard Society
PO Box 230192
Tigard, OR 97281

COMMONLY USED FLOWERING PLANTS 1845–1880

Early Spring:

Lilac
Kerria
Spirea
Camellia
Quince
Violets: white, yellow, and purple
Winter Jasmine
Wood Sorrel
Bergenia

Daffodil: Pheasant's Eye
Daffodil: Butter & Eggs
Spanish Bluebells
Bleeding Hearts
Grape Hyacinths
Snow Drops
Wallflower: Bloody Butcher
Forget-me-nots
Trillium

Mid to Late Spring:

Rose Campion
Peony
Perennial Sweet Pea

Stachys; Lamb's Ears
Roses
Iris

Clematis: Virgin's Bower   Vinca
Dianthus: Bellis Daisy
   Sweet William,
    Clove Pinks   Lily of the Valley
Hawthorne   Scotch Broom
Foxglove   Sweet Rocket

Summer:

Hardy Geraniums: Dahlias
   Herb Robert   Day Lilies
Madonna Lily   Morning Glories
Lavender   Bouncing Betty
Hydranga   Ox-Eye Daisy
Fushcia   Single Feverfew
Honeysuckle   Single Hollyhocks
Fushcia Magellanica   Calendula
Monarda   Scented Geraniums
Yarrow   Loosestrife
Evening Primrose   Lupin
Oriental Poppies   Jupiter's Beard
Spider Wort   Tratiscanthia

Late Summer to Fall:

Goldenrod   Michealmas Daisies
Chinese Lantern Plant   Tansy
Nightshade

Annuals:

Violas   Larkspur
Cosmos   White Allysum
Love-Lies-Bleeding   Petunias
Nigella   Snapdragons
Nicotiana   Bachelor Button
Larkspur   California Poppy
Marigolds   Sunflowers

BIBLIOGRAPHY AND REFERENCES

Books:

American Association of University Women Creative Writers. *Land of the Multanomahs.* Portland: Binford and Mort, 1973.

Applegate, Shannon. *Skookum: An Oregon Family's History and Lore.* New York: William C. Morrow and Company, 1990.

Batdorf, Carol. *Northwest Native Harvest.* Blaine: Hancock House Publications, Ltd., 1990.

Better Homes and Gardens Editors. *Better Homes and Gardens Heritage of America Cookbook.* Des Moines: Merideth Books, 1975.

Brown, Sanborn. *Wines and Beers of Old New England.* Hanover: University Press of New England, 1978.

Cardwell, James. *First Fruits of the Land.* Oregon Horticultural Society, 1906.

Carleton, Will. *Farm Festivals.* Harper & Bros., N.Y., 1881

Chesanov, Jeanne. *Honeysuckle Sipping.* Camden: Down East Books, 1987.

Dana, Mrs. William Starr. *How To Know The Wild Flowers: A Guide to the Names, Haunts, and Habits of our Common Wild Flowers.* New York: Charles Scribner's Sons, 1898.

Douthit, Mary O. *Souvenir of Western Women.* Anderson and Duniway, 1905.

Friedman, Ralph. *In Search of Western Oregon.* Caldwell: The Caxton Printers, Ltd., 1990.

———. *Oregon for the Curious.* Caldwell: The Caxton Printers, Ltd., 1972.

————. *Tracking Down Oregon.* Caldwell: The Caxton Printers, Ltd., 1978.

Gaston, Joseph. *Centennial History of Oregon.* Denver: Clarke Publishing, 1912.

Gibson, James. *Farming the Frontier.* University of British Columbia, 1985.Jones, Suzi and Ramsey, Jarold, editors. *The Stories we Tell.* Corvallis: Oregon State University Press, 1994.

Grafton, John. *The American West in the Nineteenth Century.* New York: Dover Publications, 1992.

Greenway, Kate. *Language of Flowers.* Orig. 1884. Reprint, Avenal: Gramercy Press, 1978.

Gunther, Erna. *Ethnobotany of Western Washington: The Knowledge and Uses of Indigenous Plants by Native Americans.* Seattle: University of Washington Press, 1945.

Hargreaves, Sheba. *Cabin At Trail's End.* Portland: Metropolitan Press, 1928.

————. *Ward of the Redskin.* Harper and Brothers, 1929.

Holmes, Kenneth. *Covered Wagon Women 1852: Diaries and Letters from the Western Trails, 1840–1890.* Spokane: Arthur H. Clark, 1986.

Jones, Pamela. *Just Weeds: History, Myths, and Uses.* Englewood Cliffs: Prentice Hall, 1991.

Kirkwood, Charlotte M. *Into The Eye of the Setting Sun.* McMinnville: Family Association of Matheney, Cooper, Hewitt, Kirkwood and Baily, 1991.

Lampman, Evelyn S. *Tree Wagon.* New York: Doubleday, 1953.

Leighton, Ann. *American Gardens of the Nineteenth Century.* Amherst: University of Massachusetts Press, 1987.

Lockley, Fred; Mike Helm, editor. *The Lockley Files, Vol. 1: Conversations With Pioneer Women.* Eugene: Rainy Day Press, 1981.

McCormick, Gail. *Our Proud Past.* Mulino, OR: Gail McCormick Publishing Company, 1992.

Morse, Alice E. *Old Time Gardens.* New York: Macmillan, 1901.

Nickey, Louise. *Cookery of the Prairie Homesteader.* Portland: Touchstone Press, 1976.

Our Garden Book. Portland: Binford and Mort, 1941.

Owens–Adair, Bethina. *Doctor Owens–Adair.* Portland: Mann and Beach Printers, *circa* 1906.

Parsons, John. *Beside The Beautiful Willamette.* Portland: Metropolitan, 1924.

Phillips, Roger and Rix, Marilyn. *Random House Book of Roses.* New York: Random House, 1988.

Proulx, Annie and Nichols, Lew. *Sweet and Hard Cider.* Pownal: Garden
     Way, 1980.
Readers' Digest Editors. *Magic and Medicine of Plants.* New York:
     Readers' Digest Association, Inc., 1986.
Smith, Helen. *With Her Own Wings.* Beattie, 1948.
Told By The Pioneers. Olympia: WPA, 1937-1938.
Wigginton, Eliot, editor. *Foxfire.* New York: Anchor Press.
Williams, Jacqueline. *Wagon Wheel Kitchens.* St. Lawrence: University
     Press of Kansas, 1993.

Interviews:

Applegate, Shannon, historian and pioneer descendant.
Applegate, Susan, historian and pioneer descendant.
Barlow House owner.
Beals, Herbert, Oregon historian and author, Gladstone, Oregon.
Bush House and Tartar Rose Gardens, Salem Oregon: Interview with
     Curator
Daley, Julie, historian, Fort Vancouver.
Dalton, James, seed historian, Oregon City, Oregon.
Dunlap, Marion, historian, pioneer descendant, and early founder of
     Home Orchard Society.
Hop Commission, staff interviews and personal accounts.
Hunsaker, Joyce, "Fanny", historian and national award winner for his-
     torical interpretation.
Igo, Mike, Botanist, Crate Point Interpretive Center, The Dalles
Mc Donald, Christa, historian, Milwaukie Museum. Milwaukie, Oregon.
Mendleson,Kathy, garden historian.
Oliver, Louise, historian, author, and pioneer descendant.
Olmstead State Park, Ellensburg, Washington, Curator.
Wilson, Nancy, historian and author, Mc Loughlin House.
Witter, Mrs., garden historian, Milwaukie, Oregon.
———. curator, W.& H. Chang Museum, John Day

Newspapers, Periodicals, and Newsletters:

Historical Gardner. Kathy Mendleson, Publisher.
Oregon City Enterprise: "Rose Farm." September 12, 1935.
Oregonian: "Roses That Bloom in History." March 26, 1939.
———. "Grandmother's Flowers." April 1909.
Oregon Journal: "Impressions and Observations," by Fred Lockley.
     October 2, 1936.
Oregon Historical Quarterly, Vol. 36. "Pioneer Rose Association."

Vickers Magazine 1888. Clackamas County Historical Society collection.
Unpublished Works:
Albro, Mary Drain,Unpublished works. Pacific University Archives, Forest Grove, Oregon.

Dalton, James, seed historian, Oregon City. Research notes.

Historical Trees and Shrubs. Oregon State Federation of Garden Clubs Bicentennial Project, 1976.

Hunsaker family, *Hunsaker Family Chronicles.* Clackamas County Historical Society.

Igo, Mike, botanist, Crate Point Interpretive Center, The Dalles. Research notes.

METRO Brief History of Lone Fir Cemetery.

Olmstead State Park, Ellensburg Washington. Curator's research and archival notes.

Oregon Historical Society, old seed lists and catalogs.

Payette National Forest staff members. Anthropological and archeological summaries.

Robison Letters. Eugene: University of Oregon Library.

Witter, Mrs., garden historian, Milwaukie, Oregon. Research notes.

Miscellaneous:
Fort Vancouver Archives.

Marylhurst Archives.

Milwaukie Museum Archives.

Oregon Historical Society, historic seed lists and catalogs.

INDEX

Albro, Mary Drain: 98-99, 101
Apples: 58, 61-62, 74, 75
Applegates: 32-33
Aurora Colony: 12, 87

Babies: 38, 44
Bachelor Buttons: 45, 47
Barlow Road: 64, 66, 67
Barlow, Sam: 67
Barlow William: 67-69
Beets: 7, 12
Bread: 24, 78
Blackberries: 33
Bleeding Hearts (Dicentra): 88
Bouncing Betty (Saponaria): 44

Cabbage: 6, 7, 23
Calendula (Pot Marigold): 54
Camas: 36-38
Camelia: 82
Cascara (Chittim Bark): 34
Cash Crops: 62, 73
Catholic: 54-55, 101
Cedar: 32, 66, 82
Cemeteries and Burial Customs:
    41, 78-82, 99, 102, 103
Chamber Pots (Thunder Mugs):
    17-19
Chamomile: 54, 84

Champoeg (French Prairie): 45-47,
    99
Cherries: 60-63
Cherry Tree: 34
Chickens: 9-11
Chickweed: 35
Chicory: 42
Children; games & treats: 4, 38-
    39, 44, 88, 96
Chinese: 17, 62
Cider: 76
Comfrey: 42
Cooking: 8, 25, 27, 28
Cottonwood (Balm of Gilliad): 36
Cucumbers: 9-11

Daylillies: 54
Dainties: 23-24, 72
Dandelions: 41, 57
Denneys: 96
Disease: 10-12, 67

Elderberry: 36

Fat: 19, 36
Fern: 38-39
Feverfew: 54
Fir: 33, 41
Flax: 19-21

Foster Farm: 65-66, 89
Foster, Phillip: 66
Fort Vancouver: 2-6, 96, 101-102
Foxglove (Digitalis): 44, 84

Garden Plans: 29, center color section following page 52
Garden Recreations: Appendix
Ginger, Wild: 38
Gingsing: 73
Grapes: 71-72
Grape Hyacinths (Muscari): 81

Harrison's Yellow Rose: 97
Hawaiian (Sandwich Islands): 3, 63
Heal All (Prunella Vulgaris): 33
Holly: 82
Holly Hocks: 90-92
Home Cures: 12-14, 33-36, 41,55
Honeysuckle: 84-86
Hops: 14-16, 24, 96
Horehound: 54, 56
Horsetail Fern (Equisetum): 38
Hudson's Bay Company: 1, 2, 7, 9
Hunsaker: 90, 101-103

Ivy: 83

Johnny Jump Ups (Violas): 54
Jonquils (Narcissus/Daffodils): 54, 79

Keil, William: 79, 85-87

Lavender: 54
Lewis and Clark: 16, 38, 43
Lilacs: 81, 82, 87, 89
Longhorns: 11, 18, 64
Luelling: 59, 65
Lunaria (Money Plant): 84

Marigold: 54
Matheney: 12, 85, 93
Doctor McLoughlin: 6, 9, 45, 59
Milk: 17-19
Miner's Lettuce (Claytonia): 34
Mint: 54
Missionary: 7, 58, 61
Moss Roses: 109
Mulberries: 19
Mullein: 40-41

Native American: 19-21, 72, 32, 35, 37-39, 41, 43, 61
Nightshade (Bittersweet): 80
Nuts: 67-70, 86

Old Cardinal Rose: 100
Onions: 2, 12
Oregon Grape: 35
Oxalis: 35

Pacific University: 98-99
Panama: 8, 67
Peach: 65-66, 84
Peony: 84, 85-87
Period Plant Lists: 119-120
Pine: 34-35, 41
Pioneer Rose Association: 99, 103-104
Plant Sources: 117-118
Plantain: 42
Plum: 62
Poppies: 45
Potatoes: 2, 7, 16-17
Pumpkin: 7, 22

Quince: 70-71

Rhubarb: 13, 62
Roses: 32-33, 78, 80, 82, 84
Rose Collecting: 99
Rose Geranium: 56

Rose List: Center Section

Sage: 13
Salves: 35
Scotch Broom: 84
Seeds: 9, 38, 77, 115, 117-118
Shepard's Purse: 38
Shipley: 71
Snowdrops (Galanthus): 79
Sorrel: 35
Sourdough: 26
Stoves: 25-27
Strawberries: 62
Sugar: 63
Sweetbriar Rose: 93-94, 96-97
Sweet Peas (perennial); 81, 84

Tansy (True): 41
Teasel: 73
Thistles: 43

Thyme: 7
Tinware: 17
Tobacco: 13
Tools: 12, 19
Trillium: 33

Vegetables: 4-5, 12, 23
Vinca (Perriwinkle): 79-80
Vinegar: 75-76
Violets: 41, 79

Washing: 44
Wheat: 9, 47
Willow: 99
Whitman, Narcissa: 6, 37

Yarrow: 34-35
Yeast: 25-27, 43
Yucca: 82